THE QUEST OF HONOR

The Quest
of Honor

By

E. BOYD BARRETT

Author of *Shepherds in the Mist,*
Life Begins With Love, etc.

THE BRUCE PUBLISHING COMPANY
MILWAUKEE

NIHIL OBSTAT:

JOHN A. SCHULIEN, S.T.D.
Censor librorum

IMPRIMATUR:

ROMAN R. ATKIELSKI, D.D.
Administrator Sede Vacante Archidioecesis Milwauchiensis

August 24, 1953

The author wishes to thank the editors of *Ave Maria, The Sign*, and *The Catholic World* for permission to re-use material which appeared in their magazines.

INTRODUCTION

I THINK I should begin the story of honor by stating two facts and expressing an opinion. The *facts* are: (1) We feel unfeigned and immense admiration for honorable conduct in others. (2) We are exceedingly "touchy" about our own honor, to the extent that we are furious if it is ever called in question. The *opinion* is that in spite of our vital interest in honor, and our intense reactions to it, most of us lack an adequate understanding of it, and our ideas about a true and complete code of honor are vague and nebulous. This book is written in order to clarify the idea of honor and to explain its implications by furnishing a practical code of honor. In it the portrait of a man of high honor is painted in thoughts and words.

There is a pretty proverb coming down from the days of chivalry: *"Los manos blancas no ofenden"* — Clean hands do no hurt. It expresses the *spirit* of honor: a delicate and constant respect for the rights and the well-being of others. The *substance,* as contrasted with the *spirit* of honor, is conveyed in another old Spanish saying: *"El dar es honor"* — Giving is honor. The noble generosity inherent in it prompts men to aid the weak, to serve those in need, to deal fairly, faithfully, and truthfully with all.

Honor is grafted in love, and love, as we know, has

roots that draw the sap of goodness from God. In honor, as in love, there is culture and refinement. "Love," said the Greeks, "teaches culture even if one was before uncultured." Love charms and endears: honor wins respect. Love "gives a relish to everything": honor cleanses and ennobles everything. Love and honor grow and wax strong together; but should the human heart harden and chill, honor dims and fades.

There are those who say that honor is valueless, "a bubble," "a mere word." They murmur cynically: "Honor buys no beef." Such men, absorbed in the pursuit of material things and of opportunity, do not want to hear a word about honor or its high purpose. Their greed for practical benefits makes them deaf. "Hungry bellies have no ears!"

Many think of honor as no more than an adornment but they gravely underestimate its value. *Honor is not only an adornment; it is a necessity.* Without honor, in an individual, or in a nation, there is moral decay. With moral decay comes loss of freedom; thereafter naught but despair remains.

If, as would seem, our national habits of honor are weakening and fading — in the market place, on the college campus, in the arena of public life shocking evidences of dishonor have appeared of late — it is all-important for us to revive our interest in honor and our devotion to it.

The man who lets go of his sense of honor lightly, as an unimportant factor in his soul, is rash to the point of folly, but it is a difficult task to show him so. The Chinese

warn us: "One has never so much need of his wit as
when he has to do with a fool."

Honor calls for deep sincerity of conduct, whether in
social or business life. Its slogan is ever: "Do on the hill
what you would do in the hall." Honor does not act
thus and so, because of onlookers. In his own conscience,
the man of honor has "a thousand witnesses." Honor faces
and performs its allotted task, not for the cheers it may
win but because it is right. Amid failures, as in success,
honor remains unchanged. *"The honorable man is always
honorable, even in misfortune,"* say the wise men of
Arabia.

Honor wears no outward garb by which it can be
recognized. Ermine does not bear witness to its presence;
often "it peereth from the meanest robe" (Shakespeare).
The man with charm, clear-eyed and steady-handed,
whose words ring true and fair, the "cynosure of every
eye," may yet be wholly wanting in honor. "Many an
apple," said the ancient, Alfred, "is bright without but
bitter within."

Though honor is a moral quality, it may be spoken
of as a weapon, an instrument wherewith to awaken awe.
It has a keen edge, but the blade is not for hurting but for
saving. The French have a subtle saying: "Who carries
a sword carries peace." Honor is that kind of sword. It is
used to prevent wrong, not to provoke it. It is a sword
that keeps other swords in their scabbards. Honor, with
"a wise thought" and a noble gesture, can allay incipient
strife and make enemies see each other as friends.

The scope of honor is wide in our personal lives. Its part is greater than to keep us from words and deeds of shame. Its most important role is to keep us from the misuse of licit things. We should not disregard the warning of moralists: *"Perimus licitis"* — We fall away by means of licit things. Through the wrong use or overuse of things that are lawful we compromise our virtue and our honor. "Who lets the devil sit on his shoulder shall have him presently sit on his head." Honor is alert to draw the line when danger is nigh. As the Scotch poet, Bobby Burns, wrote:

> Where you feel your honor grip,
> Let that aye be your border.

It is difficult, if not impossible, to do full justice to the inherent beauty of honor. There is a color, a poetry, a harmony in an act of honor one cannot describe. "You can paint the flower but you can't paint its scent." Livy, who was probably handing on a thought of Greek philosophy, said that honor was "the safest thing because it was the most beautiful thing" (*quod pulcherrimum, idem tutissimum*). In words of unequaled delicacy the Psalmist sang of "The guiltless in act, the pure in heart, one who never set his heart on lying tales, or swore treacherously to his neighbor" (Ps. 23:4). It was of the honorable one he sang.

In attempting to analyze honor and to study its many facets great help is to be found in those terse and venerable comments on men's ways and doings that we call *proverbs*. These sayings, full of insight and wit, carry the thoughts and feelings of all mankind since before the pyramids were dreamed of. Their authority is very great, for their survival is due to their truth. These revered "copper coins of human wisdom" deal directly or indirectly with honor and vindicate its nobility and worth.

> The people's voice, the voice of God we call,
> And what are proverbs but the people's voice,
> Coined first, and current made by common choice.
> Then, sure, they must have weight and truth withal!
> (Howell.)

No man should, therefore, deem it other than worth while to study honor and to cultivate it, for if he has ears he can hear the voice of the people, which represents the voice of God (*vox populi, vox Dei*), praising and commending honor.

CONTENTS

THE QUEST OF HONOR

I

THE MEANING OF HONOR

THERE is a question that a man who knows his duty should never ask: "What will people say if I do this?" Honor calls for courage and independence; it demands that a man be indifferent to what people may say or think. Honor is concerned about doing what is right, and not about winning praise. "Whether others judge well or ill of thee," says À Kempis, "thou are not on that account other than thyself."

To flatter others, to "play up to them," is no part of honor, nor is it the way of freedom and peace of mind. Unless a man "careth not to please men nor feareth to displease them" (À Kempis) his hands will soon be soiled, for there is no commoner pitfall of honor than human respect. The man who caters to others "daubs himself with sugar," only to find himself "covered with flies." The flatterer soon discovers that he is of no account and incapable of doing good. A Persian proverb conveys this truth in figurative words: "Be not all sugar or the world will gulp thee down!"

Many people attach great importance to maintaining their "personal dignity" and seek to impress others by a display of their possessions, whether material or moral. Some of them we call "stuffed shirts," men who are too grand to do this or that, to mix with or meet those whom they consider their inferiors. They act as though they belonged to a higher caste. Their mistaken honor lies in living up to their ideas of what is in accord with their so-called dignity.

In the town in Ireland where I grew up there were men, quite respectable men, of the class I have described. They were the police who patrolled the streets. They wore bright blue uniforms, with silver buttons, and helmets embossed with silver. Most of them had mustaches waxed to saber points, and their black shoes always shone. Their hands were gloved in white. These policemen were very conscious of their dignity, their "honor" they would have called it, and they showed it in a remarkable way. Never, under any circumstances, even when pursuing a thief, would they break into a run. They would remove their gloves, walk fast, but run — never!

The Arabs hand down a story proverb that refers to this false idea of honor. It is told thus. "They said to the camel bird (the ostrich), 'Carry!'; it answered, 'I cannot; I am a bird.' They said 'Fly!'; it answered, 'I cannot; for I am a camel!'"

People are fond of showing off their clothes, their

antiques, their cars, with a view to impressing others and enhancing their honor. As they point to this or that they boast with "the impudence of a dog on his own dunghill." They go to no end of trouble to draw attention to the beauty of their home, though, as an old proverb has it: "A man may love his house well without riding on the ridge." All their geese are swans; "their frogs are goddesses."

Does a name add to one's honor? Many people have the strange delusion that it does. If they have a name with a hint of celebrity in it, they are very insistent that it should be spelled and pronounced correctly. Not a few people change their names to something that sounds better, if they are dissatisfied with what they have. There is a story of an Indian who did not like his name, which was "Rain-in-the-face," and who went to the judge to get another better-sounding one. When the judge asked him what new name he preferred, he answered: "Drizzlepuss."

There are many who think that honor is enhanced, not only by displays of pride, but by displays of cruelty and injustice. The ruling race or caste rides roughly on the necks of underdogs as though honor required it. The idea that "might makes right" gives rise to the identification of outrage with honor. The sad-souled Bengalese, victims of many ages of injustice, pass on the saying: "Who gives blows is a master; who gives none is a dog." How seldom have colonial rulers understood and practiced the honor implicit in St. Paul's command: "Do good to all men!"

In slighting remarks and in name-calling in its many

phases we see other attempts to reach honor by riding on the back of cruelty. The man or woman who utters a cutting remark about another thinks that he or she gains prestige for the cleverness of the bitter word. Though "sisters under the skin," the colonel's lady belittles Judy O'Grady — but what does her witticism amount to? When "one ass names another 'Long Ears,'" does he grow in honor by so doing? Honor is not won by despising our brothers and our sisters.

Few of us are conscious of the lesser dishonors in our conduct. We like to boast about our honor, and there is frequently on our lips the phrase, "I'd be ashamed to do such a thing!" The presence of honor is not proved by sounds but by deeds. "Not everyone who blows a horn is a huntsman." To boast of our honor is to loosen hold of it. Many no doubt have read the saying of Emerson about one who was proclaiming how honorable he was: "The louder he talked of his honor, the faster we counted our spoons."

Though good in itself, and in a sense necessary, personal ambition is a common pitfall of honor. While it is commendable for us to develop to the full the gifts and opportunities that God has given us, we have to beware, in so doing, of developing an egotistic and selfish habit of living. Selfishness discounts charity and the rights and interests of others. Selfishness leads to hurting and wronging others, and negates honor completely in the end.

But even though personal ambition need not turn into selfish conduct, it is calculated to bring about conflicts with honor. Take the question of leadership, for example. In our ambition we usually seek the position of leader. We are not likely to take a thorough course in obedience and in doing lowly duties as a necessary preparation for the post of command, although it is said with truth: "He that cannot obey, cannot command." In our fervent ambition to reach the top, we dispense with learning to play second fiddle.

Does it occur to us, in our ambition to lead others, that those whom we wish to lead might make better captains than ourselves? All cannot be leaders; some must be left to do the drudgery. "If I am master, and you are master, who shall drive the ass?" Actually, from the point of view of true honor, to drive an ass is as worthy as to give orders. When stout men (that is, gallant warriors) find that their ambitions conflict, where lies the path of honor? "You stout, and I stout, and who'll carry the dirt out?"

There is current the false idea that when ambition is disappointed — by failure in an examination or loss in a battle — there is disgrace. The phrase "no substitute for victory" represents a common thought, a thought to be repudiated. There can be high honor in defeat. We may "lose our boots without losing our spurs." We may *deserve* success, we may *merit* it fully, without having it; and it is axiomatic that honor lies in merit. Can we say that there was "no substitute for victory" at Thermopylae? Was not Leonidas' defeat a greater thing than victory? Wrote Samuel Butler, in witty doggerel:

He that is valiant, and dares fight,
Tho' drubbed can lose no honor by't (*Hudibras*).

While personal ambition may prove, at times, a stumbling block in the way of honorable conduct, personal modesty is an essential requirement of honor. To be honorable a man needs humility; he needs to see his own weakness and limitations. St. Augustine used to pray: "Free me from that evil man — from myself." The modest man prays in like fashion. He knows that "No man has a worse friend than he brings with him from home." He knows that we are all doomed to keep bad company. No doubt, "It's better to ride alone than have a thief's company"; but we have no choice. The thief is always with us, and that is the reason why honor presents difficulties. However, we can manage to keep an eye on "the thief," and if we are humble we keep a sharp eye on him.

If we are humble we will not ask others to do the hard jobs, the dirty work; we will not "draw the snake from the hole with another man's hand." Humility aims at no special privilege. It does its fair share and "toes the line" in straight democratic fashion. The humble man seeks no exemptions; he does not place burdens on others that his own shoulders should carry. He does his part without asking others to do it for him — an admirable quality that Spaniards inculcate in a quaint way: "Let him who has a mouth not say to another, 'Blow!'"

The most treacherous arena for honor is the business world. Here honor finds its severest test. Honor demands more than keeping within the law; it calls for more than commutative justice; it insists that love as well as honest scales enter into dealings. In business men are wont "to cut broad thongs from other men's leather," but in so doing they overreach. The warning of St. Paul is the main-stay of honor in business: "Let no man over-reach or circumvent his brother in business." A man who is over-eager for profit puts his own honor in danger. The saying, "Honor and profit will not keep in one sack," is cynical, but a man can avoid "smart practices," keep well in mind the rights of others to a completely fair deal, and still make a profit. *It is the intemperate love of riches that leads to dishonor and misfortune!* "He who will be rich in a year, at the half-year they hang him."

I had, on one occasion, a business deal with a cobbler in an Irish village, which I consider a classic example of honor in trade. I was driving a new American sports-model car with a quarrelsome companion beside me, my Kerry Blue. I needed a muzzle, and wanted one that could be adjusted. I tried everywhere, in vain, to get what I wanted, and then, passing through this village, I saw a cobbler's shop and thought I'd try my luck there. I stopped my car in front and entered. A tall, spare man at work at a bench looked up and asked me with a quiet smile what I needed. I told him how anxious I was to get an adjustable muzzle for my dog, and how I had failed to get one "for love or money." He listened, amused, to my story, and said: "I think I can make one for you."

He went to work at once, cutting a strip of excellent leather from a hide that hung on his wall. Then he began to shape the muzzle. Meanwhile, he glanced outside and saw my car. "A 'yank,'" he thought, "plenty rich, and like all of them in a mighty hurry!" I was thinking: "I'll have to pay for this through the nose!"

Soon the muzzle was made. It was what I wanted. It was strong, light, and beautifully finished. I admired it and asked: "How much?"

He looked at me steadily. "Sixpence" — fifteen cents!

"That's ridiculous!" I burst out. "It's worth at least five shillings!"

He shook his head, smiling. "No, sir. Sixpence is my price; but thank you."

I was caught in a deep sense of shame. Who was I to attempt to interfere with the way an honorable man conducted his affairs? How cheap I was, with my implied flattery! Here was the rare kind of honesty that refuses to be opportunist. What deep insight there lies in the age-old proverb: "Mock not a cobbler for his black thumbs!"

There are, of course, standards and grades of honor. That honor, I take it, is higher which shows more concern for human rights than for property rights. By the same token, there is more dishonor in injuring a person than in stealing his goods.

We consider, for example, two college girls, Doris and Betty. Doris goes into a friend's room in her absence, reads her private letters, and her secret diary, and steals some of her trinkets. She is mean, a thief, and if she is ever found out, she will be despised and disgraced.

Betty, who owns a car, drives a party of girl friends

to a roadhouse where they indulge freely in cocktails. Back in the car again, Betty in a half-tipsy state takes the wheel and careens along the highway. Such a drive, dangerous and crazy though it be, is great fun until it ends in a tragic smashup, or until, as can happen, the car is safely parked and the girls all emerge uninjured.

But what of the shame and dishonor of the escapade? Betty's sin against honor was as grievous as could be. She put in jeopardy the lives of others, their most sacred rights. Doris' sin was bad enough but it was much less, for she only stole a few secrets and trinkets. On the campus, were the facts about Doris and Betty known, Betty's crime would be laughed off, but Doris' fault would be universally condemned. College boys and girls have little understanding of the true nature of honor.

The source of much dishonor in America is the force and prevalence of the gang spirit. Americans like to belong to a party, to go along with it, and to let party leaders do their thinking for them. When a quarrel or mêlée arises, without considering the *pros* or *cons,* the right or wrong of the dispute, the average American pitches in to fight alongside his friends. He justifies himself by the sophism that he must keep faith with the party, or that he must not split its ranks.

Such a mentality is not good enough for a man of honor. Honor calls for a higher code of conduct than that of "follow the leader" blindly. Honor expects of us, as free men, to "use our heads," and to assure ourselves that an act or a policy is right before we commit ourselves to it.

Should we "howl with wolves" and join them in devouring the lamb, because it happens that the wolves are our friends?

Does it not often happen that, with little information to guide us, and without a complete knowledge of the facts of the case, we join the mob in defaming and discrediting someone, be he a public or a private figure? The man whom we condemn unheard may be wholly innocent of the charges preferred against him. His inner honor may be, unlike ours, intact. Yet we take sides against him. "Detraction," wrote Shakespeare, does not suffer honor "to live with the living." In detraction there is sadism; in honor there is none.

There is an old proverb, which, at first sight, is likely to shock, but when understood, its wisdom is appreciated. It is to be found among the thirteenth-century *Proverbs of Hendyng* and reads: "Wel fyht that wel flyth" — He fights well that flies well. What is the meaning of this seemingly defeatist aphorism?

It often happens that a man in some public place is subjected to a slighting remark or a deliberate act of rudeness. In fear that onlookers may think him "yellow" if he swallows the insult, he doubles his fists and strikes — "to vindicate his honor." In his stupidity he believes that he has no alternative but to retaliate with violence to avenge the wrong done him. This shabby form of dueling "is not an institution of honor but a horrible and barbarous custom which a courageous man despises and a good man abhors" (Rousseau).

How shallow is the philosophy, how weak the religious spirit of the man who believes in revenge! In an act of revenge, or retaliation (to use a milder word that cloaks the same ugliness), a man gives free rein to pride, hate, and intolerance. In his passion "he rides a mad horse." Thinking that the insult is a heinous wrong (because he is the victim of it), he lashes out to repay it with a greater wrong.

But *"he fights well that flies well,"* that forgives and repays an unwarranted insult with patience and tolerance. "To forgive is the noblest vengeance," and the only kind of vengeance in accord with honor and right reason. In forgiveness there is a moral loveliness that Indian sages dwell upon in a charming way. "The sandal tree," they say, "perfumes the ax that fells it."

It is no doubt difficult, if not impossible, to eradicate from the minds of men the delusion that there is an essential nexus between honor and fighting. In a vein of silly sentiment, Tennyson makes Sir Gallahad boast:

"My bright sword carves the casques of men"

as though there were honor in slaughter! In itself, fighting, unless it be the stern duty of a citizen, is foul and foolish. Every blow a man delivers against a brother is a curse, and as the Turks tell: "Curses like chickens come home to roost." The quarrelsome man has no happy homecoming: "The tulying (fighting) dog comes halting home." It is in spreading peace and working for peace that honor lies. The greatest of all teachers, Christ, the divine Teacher, brought a message of peace and forgiveness and our honor lies in obeying His teaching.

In summing up our thoughts on the meaning of honor, we find that honor has no essential connection with success, prosperity, glory, or proud insistence upon personal rights. It can flourish amid poverty, failure, ignorance, and the anonymity of the cloister. It is "a spur that pricks" the mind of a cobbler as well as a king. While it calls for independence of mind and moral courage it has also "the finest sense of justice."

Many have written of honor. In his fine poem, "Character of the Happy Warrior," Wordsworth has painted in detail a portrait of a man of honor who "keeps faithful with a singleness of aim"; who cherishes "the law of reason"; "whose high endeavors are an inward light" —

> Whom neither shape of danger can dismay,
> Nor thought of tender happiness betray.

Yet, while much has been written in praise of honor, there is no accepted definition of it to be found.

We come closest to the inner nature of honor when we interpret it as *concern about the rights of others.* It is an unselfish virtue; it is inspired by love; and it has to do with social living, though it belongs both to hill and hall.

Still, it is not enough for us to grasp the inner meaning of honor; understanding without love is only half possession. Our hearts must embrace honor warmly and loyally, and our emotion must be kindled by dwelling on "what-

soever things are true . . . whatsoever just . . . whatsoever
lovely . . . whatsoever of good fame" (St. Paul).

> Man with his burning soul
> Has but an hour of breath,
> To build a ship of truth,
> In which his soul may sail (John Masefield).

CHAPTER

II

USE YOUR HEAD!

IN MANY stories that Christ told us we find the lesson that it is right to be prudent, namely, "to use our heads." The most notable of these stories is that of the Five Wise and Five Foolish Virgins. The former had foresight and took along with their lamps a surplus of oil, in case of mishap or delay. They had the good sense and firmness not to part with their oil. Christ praised and rewarded them in the story; the others He blamed and punished. Christ wanted us to see that: "It is through lack of thinking that many men are undone." From His lips issued the pointed counsel: "Sit down and think!" "Sit down and reckon the charges!"

Foresight, prudence (from the Latin word *providere*, "to foresee"), was regarded by Greek philosophers as a virtue. Plato called it "the chief and leader" of the virtues. Aristotle, who also placed it first, defined it as "right reason applied in practical affairs." Later, Christian philos-

ophers, adopting much of Greek thought on the *natural*
virtues, named four of them — prudence, justice, temperance, and fortitude — *cardinal virtues,* because they were
common qualities of all the moral virtues and served as
hinges for them.

The reason prudence is placed first among virtues, by
Aquinas and others, is that other virtues are not possible
without it as concomitant. Courage, divorced from prudence, becomes foolhardiness; temperance becomes fanaticism; charity becomes wastefulness. Prudence, thus,
has empire over other virtues and is in that sense more
important than any of them.

Prudence points out "what course of action to take in
any round of concrete circumstances." Always necessary,
it is, as Molière said, "always in season." It is defined as
"an intellectual habit that enables us to see, in any given
juncture of human affairs, what is right to do, and what
is wrong to do; how to come at the one and to avoid the
other." Prudence casts about for the means to reach its
aim; it judges of the fitness of the means; it calls for the
employment of the right means.

It is not surprising that the rules of prudence find a
place in folklore and literature. Knowing, as Juvenal
writes, that "one has no protecting power save prudence,"
people keep reminding themselves of its importance. The
need of foresight, in deed and word, is most frequently
taught:

> Look e'er you leap, see e'er you go,
> It may be to your profit so!

And when you speak, think twice in advance. "To speak without thinking," say the Spaniards, "is to shoot without looking."

When we have something to do, be it only to plant a fruit tree or make a box, we should "sit down and think," so that we may do our job right. We fall into all kinds of mistakes unless we plan ahead. As the poet Denham wrote:

> When any great design thou dost intend,
> Think on the means, the manner and the end.

Usually it is as easy to do a thing right as to do it wrong; if we do it wrong we may have to do it over again — if it can be redone — at considerable personal cost.

On one occasion I had to cut down an oak tree that was growing on the side of a hill, very close to the top. I needed the trunk and branches for firewood, and I knew that if I cut and sawed the tree at the wrong place, instead of falling upward, it would fall the other way and roll down the hill. There was a little problem of thinking and searching to be done to find "the wise thought" about where to use my ax and saw. I knew that "one wise thought is better than many hands," but I was impatient. It's an old saying that "a dog that trots about finds a bone," but my mind was too lazy to trot about in search of what I needed — the right idea.

Taking a chance, I started in. In due time the oak tree began to topple; like a tired giant it slowly fell — down the hill it fell, rolling over and over, until it reached the bottom!

Francis Bacon once uttered a word that applies to folk who rush into doing things without knowing what they're doing. He said sagely: "He that cannot see well, let him go softly."

In many of our undertakings we cannot count on getting a second chance. What we do is done for all time, and there is no way of doing it over again. *We should do things right at the first attempt.* It is all-important to take the greatest pains to avoid a wrong start. "Measure thy cloth ten times," warns a Russian proverb, "thou canst cut it but once."

Though life is a much more complex game than chess, we find in this game of skill an admirable illustration of the great need of prudence and foresight.

Before every move in the game we must study the probable consequences. We must, as far as possible, anticipate the plan of our adversary. No move should be purposeless; either it should advance attack or strengthen defense. *A wasted move may mean a lost game.* If our opponent is allowed to build up too strong an attack, our belated defense may be useless. "Precaution is better than cure." Should we gain the upper hand, and have victory, seemingly, within reach, we must still beware. Many a "sure" victory is forfeited through overconfidence. "Call me not olive till you see me gathered," say the Spaniards. Not until nighttime should we "praise a fair day."

Sometimes at chess, as we do in life, we pursue our purpose with too much zest and eagerness. In so doing we may fall into a trap. All may seem to be going well, but we must not overextend ourselves.

> With more than a propitious gale,
> Take half thy canvas in! (Horace.)

Besides epitomizing the rules of prudence, the game of chess supplies an insight into the psychology of prudence. It throws light on the fact that one's prudence seems to vary in amount from day to day. On one day a man will play good chess; on another day his game will be poor.

One reason for this variation is *fatigue*. A chess player may be unconsciously tired. Prudence belongs to the brain and fatigue hinders brainwork. It is wise to avoid important decisions when one is fagged. Often when we think we are thinking, we are not thinking at all.

Another cause of faulty chess playing is *excitement*. When a player gets worked up or excited, he is likely to overlook something that he should take into account. To think clearly we need to keep cool, "to take things by their smooth handle" (Jefferson). When excited several ideas assail us and we attempt many things. How contrary to this is the wise proverb of Portugal: "Think of many things; do only one!"

Defeatism is another cause of bad play. When a chess player allows himself to be overawed by the skill of his opponent, he is doomed. He misses opportunities of attack, or he retreats precipitately. Prudent conduct calls for confidence, for the will to succeed. "Them ez will, kin" is an Americanism that serves to translate the Latin adage: *"Fac velis, perficies"* — Make yourself want to succeed, and you will succeed!

It goes without saying that *ill temper* is an obstacle to prudent conduct. Prudence sees an enemy rather than a friend in anger. "You win by prudence rather than by ire." Nor is wine an auxiliary of wisdom and foresight. Its function is "to gladden the heart" rather than to energize thinking. It is no new discovery that "Counsel over cups is crazy!"

Whatever its source, *impulsiveness*, hasty eagerness to get things done, is the subtlest foe of prudence. Often we are unaware of the presence of impulse in our make-up. We take ourselves to be self-controlled, restrained, where-as we are in fact "itchy to get going." We are satisfied that our vision is clear and sure and calm, but, mostly, we deceive ourselves. Until we are really and sincerely hospitable to *second thoughts;* until we act in accord with the principle: "He thinks not well who thinks not again," we remain impulsive.

If we recall again, for a moment, the parable of the Wise and Foolish Virgins, we notice that fifty per cent of them failed "to use their heads." We may not, of course, conclude from this that Christ taught that half the world is given to folly, but we may conclude that fools are not rare.

It is the thought of mankind that fools are to be found

everywhere. Like weeds, they grow without watering. "If folly were a pain," says a proverb, "there would be crying in every house." There would be crying not only in houses, but in colleges and laboratories of science as well. Does it not happen to our certain knowledge that men, famous and conspicuous in one department of learning, bray like asses when they discuss matters beyond their ken? Aptitude in one science fails to qualify a man to speak with competence in another, totally alien, science. A good mathematician is not, by virtue of his equations, fit to teach history, or theology. Is there not wit and wisdom in the Spanish saw: *"Tonto sin saber latin, nunca es gran tonto"* — A fool, unless he know Latin, is never a great fool!

Many people employ their *feeling* as a guide instead of their head. Feeling, for them, is a mixture of impulse and hunch, a kind of spontaneous intuition. As a guide this feeling is not wholly blind. It draws to some extent on experience, but at best it is unreliable. It is a very different mental operation from "sitting down and reckoning the charges," as Christ told us to do.

There are people who take it for granted that their emotions do not fail them and who allow themselves to be carried away on a flood of emotion. Sometimes an emotion may be creditable, but not for that reason should it be taken as guide. As an example, familiar to Catholics, there is the man or woman who, in the chapel, moans and groans and gives way to overdemonstrative acts of piety. I have seen a devout woman, of immense proportions, opening the sanctuary gate, striding around the sanctuary kissing all the statues, and then with a large crucifix in hand pass up the aisle blessing everyone she passed. On leaving the chapel, she still held her crucifix aloft and went on blessing all passers-by, not forgetting those who drove past in public buses! Emotions, allowed to run riot, without regard to prudence, are disturbing to others and offend against charity. Molière was right: "Prudence is always in season."

It must not be thought, however necessary prudence may be, that of itself it is sufficient for the good life. Far from it! Prudence has only to do with the mind, not with the will. It is in the will that right action is initiated. A man may be thoughtful, watchful, calculating, and yet wholly wanting in virtue. He may see what is best but do what is worst. *"Video meliora proboque, deteriora sequor"* — I see and approve the better course; I follow the worse. Such is "the wisdom of the flesh" of which St. Paul spoke; it is the antithesis of virtue. *"By skill and fraud,"* Italians say *"one can live half a year; by fraud and skill one can live the remainder."* But, in the end, justice catches up with rogues, however smart they be. "Those who swim on sin, shall sink in sorrow."

Often in life we feel a great need of guidance and of light. "We have but little light in us" (À Kempis), and we find it insufficient. Instinctively we turn to the Holy Spirit, the eternal source of light, and we pray: *"Veni lumen cordium"* — Come, Light of our hearts! Our prayer will not remain unanswered, but we may find that our doubts as to the right course of action continue. There is no miraculous lifting of the veil as yet.

It occurs to us, perhaps, to seek advice from others, and in so searching the minds of others we are still "using our heads." From whom are we to get the best advice? Surely not from those who live on offal. "He that takes the raven for guide shall light upon carrion." *The one whose advice we ask must be competent;* also he must be honest and disinterested. Virtue alone does not qualify a person to give good counsel; more than virtue is required in a confessor; understanding and experience are called for. On the other hand, one takes a risk in seeking the guidance of one who has no regard for virtue. "It is a foolish sheep that makes the wolf his confessor!"

If prudence is called for in seeking advice, when doubts and clouds obscure our vision, prudence is called for still more in the giving of advice. Though we all like to give advice, few of us are competent to do so. Often we do cruel wrong by the silly, ill-considered advice we proffer. Why have we not the good sense and humility to warn the one that seeks our counsel: "My grasp of your problem is very imperfect — my experience is very limited — my judgment is very poor. I'd like to help but fear I am unable. If you like I'll discuss your problem with you — but you will take a terrible risk if you take me for your guide!"

All of us can help, by sympathy and by a painstaking effort to see clearly the difficulty that faces another. For love's sake we can devote time — and even research — to the discussion of the other's problem. Such co-operation is honorable and wise. But when we dare to "lay down the law" for another, just because we enjoy doing so, or just because we have a high esteem for our own judgment, we betray another's rights and act dishonorably. There is, however, an exception to be made in this matter. There is one piece of counsel that can always be given with confidence, though it should be given with modesty and tact. That advice is to seek divine help through prayer.

One morning, as the sun rose, I lay sleepless in bed, still victim of a little illness, my mind occupied with the thoughts that I was writing. Then, of a sudden, the window shade to my right let in a strong, straight shaft of light — *lucis radium!* It fell on a dark spot of my room, illuminating it. At once I thought of that dark spot as a human mind receiving a gift that the Father of the Poor loves to give, that He will not refuse if asked.

When we give advice to another, do we really care whether the outcome be good or ill?

I look down from where I sit writing on a California hilltop, on fields and grassy spaces between oak groves. At one place I had been *advised* to plant a little vineyard. At another I was counseled to plant cherry trees. Another place I was told was excellent for apple trees. But what did my wise (and experienced) farmer friends care? Every bit of advice they gave went sour! Vines — cherries — apples, all failed! It was the worst things, not the best, that I was told to do!

There is no honor in trying experiments on others. If we insist on experimenting let us do so at our own risk. Perhaps some gray-haired reader will recall, as I do, a curious kind of experiment that individual Japanese soldiers tried during their attack on Port Arthur long ago. When he found a Russian shell that had not exploded the inquisitive Japanese soldier would take a hammer and tap it, good and strong, to find out whether or not it was a dud. In such a search for new knowledge the cost was not paid for by a neighbor!

There is a kind of short cut to solving a problem and discovering the right thing to do. It consists in asking oneself, while thinking of some wise and good man: "What would he do in these circumstances?" This method of problem-solving is described by Jonathan Swift, in characteristic doggerel:

> In points of honor to be try'd,
> All passions should be laid aside;
> Ask no advice, but think alone,
> *Suppose the question not your own.*
> "How shall I act?" is not your case,
> But "How would Brutus in my place?"
> "In such a cause would Cato bleed?"
> And, "How would Socrates proceed?"

In the course of life we gain in experience but few of us cull from experience the wisdom that is its content. We "crack the shell but lose the kernel." Again and again we make the same mistakes. We seem incapable of learning. What is it that, to use a vulgarism, "keeps us from growing up"?

There are, no doubt, many factors that stand in the way of acquiring wisdom, but one worth dwelling upon is that referred to by Swift in the lines quoted above: "All passions should be laid aside." *We are blinded by our prejudices and our passions.* Bias makes the mind dim and murky. It is not for feebleness of mental vision that we fail to grasp truth, but on account of concealed hatred of it. We pay lip service to tolerance — there is no one but does so — but we should take it for granted that intolerances will survive within us until our dying day. Our job, during life, is to extract and squelch them one by one. The task is not easy! A bias — a passion is a fog — a dense one — and as the Japanese say: "A fog is never dispelled by a fan."

The rule of conduct — "Use Your Head!" — is the first rule of honor, because honor is grounded in reasonable conduct. Were honor a mere emotion or impulse it would not be necessary to "use our heads" in order to attain to honor. But honor is a principle, and *the mind must be in control where and when one has to do with honor.*

Without "reckoning the charges," without "sitting down to think," we cannot fulfill the various material and spiritual obligations that honor imposes upon us. How, to take a plain example, can we meet all our debts, promptly and fully, and keep all our promises to the letter, unless we "use our heads" to good purpose? How, without giving thought to it, can we keep in mind and respect the rights of others? Yet this task is the first obligation of honor.

The portrait of a man of honor is not that of a gallant knight shattering casques in a tournay to the applause of fair maidens, but rather that of a man who sits, quiet and pensive, planning with care how to meet his obligations.

CHAPTER

III

PLAY IT FAIR!

A CHILD can't spell the word *justice* but he'll cry out: "No fair!" when he feels that he's not getting his rights. To play fair is a homely synonym for being just, for respecting the rights of others, whatever they may be.

Alexander Hamilton made emphatic use of the word *sacred* when he wrote: "The sacred rights of man are not to be rummaged from among old parchments or musty records. They are written, as with a sunbeam, in the whole volume of human nature by the hand of Divinity Itself and can never be erased." These rights are dear to us and precious in proportion as we understand them. They constitute our bread ticket, our foothold in life. Without them we should be hungry and homeless. They are the foundation of our well-being and our happiness. They are common to us all; none of us has a monopoly of them; there is no man who breathes but is in possession of them.

29

"We cannot suppose," wrote Henry George, "that some men have a right to be in this world, and others no right." Only then are rights enjoyed by us in an honorable way, when we grasp the fact, and act up to it, that they are truly and really common to all men.

The fundamental natural rights of man are based on the destiny and needs of human nature, as created by God. They are primordial, and they antecede the State, which is set up by man. They inhere in man's person and can neither be given nor taken away. "*A right*," declared Hugo Grotius, "*is a moral quality annexed to the person,* justly entitling him to possess some particular privilege, or to perform some particular act." A right, to quote a legal maxim, "sometimes sleeps, but it never dies." Its inalienability is familiar to us through the immortal words: "All men are endowed by their Creator with inalienable rights; among these are life, liberty, and the pursuit of happiness."

Once, I stood looking up at the ruins of a Norman castle, built on a riverbank, near a ford, in the west of Ireland. What remained of the massive walls betokened the pride and strength that the fortress once enjoyed. Over the arch of the entrance gate there was written what seemed to be an aggressive threat: "By God of Might, I hold my Right."

Was that motto a threat? Could it not be used, with becoming mildness and modesty, by a child refusing to surrender its toy to the rapacious hand of a bully? Is it not true that each one of us (the poor and weak among us as well as the more fortunate) enjoys his right to respect and consideration, as did the baron master of the Irish castle, in virtue of God's might?

It is "By God of Might" that all of us hold our rights, great or small, and those who infringe them are no friends of God.

Justice is defined as "the moral quality or habit which perfects the will and inclines it to render to each and all what belongs to them." In simpler language, using the exact words of Cicero: *"The aim of justice is to give to everyone his due."* This too is the grand aim of honor, always to "play it fair," taking no mean advantage, treating all alike, generously and sensitively seeking to respect the rights of others — to "honor all men."

There is an old saying: "When you grind your corn, give not the flour to the devil and the bran to God." It means, of course, that when we are considering the rights of others, we should put the claims of God first. The just man says, "Right's right, and fair's fair," and he knows that it is neither right nor fair to forget God or to put Him in the second place.

The just man is blind, and it is his glory so to be. His eyes are tight shut to his own personal interests. *His likes and dislikes are invisible to him.* He weighs things evenly, without knowing what lies in either scale. The smile that coaxes is lost upon him. He judges what is just objectively and renders justice, "truth in action." In his dealings with his fellows he has only one ideal, the ideal of honor, to "play it fair."

The study of justice, though it be fascinating, is not,

of course, the purpose of this chapter. Neither is it our purpose to treat in detail of the virtue of honesty, though honesty is so closely allied with honor in everyday life. All we propose to do is to touch lightly on some aspects of the fairness and unfairness that we display in our dealings with our neighbors as we live from day to day.

To begin with, *it is impossible for us to play straight with others unless we are sincere.* Our love for others must be authentic, not simulated. Our niceness should rise from the heart. "It is not with saying 'Honey! Honey!' that sweetness comes into the mouth." Warm handclasps and fond kisses need not mean a thing. As the adage goes: "A dog and a cat may kiss yet be none the better friends."

We wrong others, and that seriously, when by smiles and flattery we lead them to think that we cherish their friendship; whereas, in reality, we are encumbered by it. The day may come when they need help, and count on us to give it, only to discover that we are unwilling to inconvenience ourselves for them. *While it is an admirable thing to imitate the kind ways of generous hearts, it is an ugly thing to counterfeit them!*

There is no make-belief about honesty. It must be genuine and durable. It must survive, unscathed, when there is an opportunity to steal. It is not enough to be honest the way a cat is "when the meat is on the hook." He is not honest who, while guiltless of grand larceny, pilfers in small ways. Nor is he honest who devises a pretext for taking things that are not his and refuses to recognize himself as a thief. Such is the manner of a cat "that shuts its eyes while it steals cream."

There is an old proverb that says: "Of all kinds of men the most hanged are thieves." It means that thieving is the most common of crimes, and certainly if we put a broad meaning on the word "thief" we cannot deny its truth. To cheat at cards, to "copy" in an examination, to accept a bribe when in office, to lay claim to some experience or accomplishment of which one is not possessed — all of this is thieving. The boy who uses another's car without definite permission, the girl who puts on another girl's fur coat unknown to her, the lady who wears a hat or dress sent to her "on approval" by a store — one and all are thieves. The boy, the girl, and the lady alike violate the rights of others. They fail "to play fair."

A boy who copies in an examination does not do so to hurt other examinees, but only to gain a personal advantage. But, in effect, he does wrong to others. If successful, he steals a place in the list of those who have passed, back-rating those that are behind him. His conduct is liable to discredit the validity of the exam as a whole. He injures the morale of the honest students, who cannot but suspect that he has cheated. There is neither fairness nor prudence in what he does and the risk he takes of being disgraced is considerable. The fate of a copier is foreshadowed in a Spanish adage: "Who arrays himself in other men's garments is stripped in the middle of the street."

One of our most common forms of dishonorable conduct is that of causing pain to others by sarcasm and jokes that make a butt of others. There is no one who does not resent being the object of ridicule. The joke may be "true," but even "true jokes" are bad, for they inflict an injury. "He makes a foe who makes a jest." Why do we like to hurt people? Why do we insist on saying the bitterest things we can think of? "God does not hurt with both hands," but we inflict all the pain we can. We have no inherent right to torture others with the lash of our tongues and the saber thrusts of our venom. When we utter a bitter jest it can never be unsaid, never recalled: "A word and a stone when discharged never come back again."

The way of "fair play" is the way of mercy and of understanding. We should not ever expect too much from others, or look for perfection in their conduct. We should not expect "better bread than can be made of wheat." We will be far less inclined to fall into an angry, critical habit of mind, if we grow indulgent toward the defects and failures of others.

The habit of putting blame on others, the itch to discover where others are at fault, is little to our credit. There is meanness in it and cowardice. Our latent purpose is to put another in the wrong; all we have to do is to light upon some fault or mistake of his, and that is not difficult. "Who wishes to beat a dog, easily finds a stick." Often we are so unjust as to blame one person for the misconduct of another. "The tongue offends: the ears get a cuffing." It happens so often in life, private as well as public, that the real malefactor is suffered to go free, while the stooge is chastised. The ancients have epitomized such unreason and injustice in the adage: "The dog bites the stone that is thrown at him."

In general we are sufficiently respectful of the rights of the strong, of those who are capable of taking care of themselves; but are we not prone to do violence to the rights of little people, the feeble, the foolish, and the weak?

The rights of the underdog are, as we have seen, as sacred and as important as the rights of the overlords, but it is a truth that we are inclined to forget. We should make laws for ourselves, as the State makes laws for all citizens, the purpose of which would be "to protect the rights of the poor." Were love more abundant such laws would be needless. *"Amor regge, senza legge"* — Love rules without law.

It is easy to outsmart a "sucker" in business, to "overreach" him, but it is not the way of honor to do so. It is easy to take advantage of another's ignorance or incompetence, but again, it is dishonorable to do so. In no respect does the standard of honor contrast so startlingly with the world's standard as in this matter of respecting the rights of the weak.

Not long ago, when listening to a radio show, I heard an announcer questioning an old Canadian barber: "How did you learn your trade in those days?" The barber answered: "We used to take poor kids off the street and put them in our chairs and practice on them!" As he spoke an Arabian proverb came to my mind: "The barber learns his art on the orphan's face!"

Often it happens that a housewife employs an immigrant whose knowledge of English (as well as her knowledge of current rates of pay and work conditions) is very limited, and drives her hard, making a veritable drudge of her. Because of her moral power over the poor woman, she does what she likes with her. She never thinks that might is not a source of right! She even flatters herself that she is a benefactress! When her friends call she boasts, with a wink, of her cleverness. But is she really clever? *"It is often that ye cat winks when her eye is out!"*

There are men, and women too, who ride roughshod over others, defaming them, and outwitting them in social and business affairs. They shoulder their way through life, roughly and discourteously pushing others aside as though they counted for nothing. Insistent on their own rights and privileges, they press on eagerly and rapaciously to gain their ambitions, indifferent to the sufferings and losses of others. With violence they make ample room for themselves, only to find themselves alone. Discontented at heart, they find no easy chair, nor any peace. But the thorns they sow they will yet tread on with bare feet! The ashes they cast without ruth will fly back in their own faces!

The man who has no regard for the feelings or rights of others wins no respect and inspires no trust. There is no good but only evil in him; no honor but only dishonor. In such a one no honesty is to be expected, nor generosity, nor even hospitality. A grim proverb warns: "He that eats with the devil hath need of a long spoon."

It is part of the true spirit of democracy to accord to every man a fair chance, to give "every guy a break." It is contrary to the democratic way to discriminate against anyone, whether on account of creed or color or social status. The individual, whatever his idea may be, gets a hearing and the right to make good. "One man in the right will finally get to be a majority," wrote Bob Ingersoll. And, implicit in the doctrine of democracy lies the teaching that it is wrong to interfere with others when they are acting in accord with their just rights. In effect, among other things, democracy says: "Don't interfere!"

To interfere in the affairs of others, however good our intention may be, is to assume a right that is in no way ours. It is true that when we exercise a right we harm no one (*qui jure suo utitur neminem laedit*), but when we act without a right to do so we are as likely to do harm as good. When we interfere with others, uninvited, we are almost certain to work ill. You may see another giving a bountiful gift and question his rectitude. If so, what will he say to you? "Is it not lawful for me to do as I will? Is thy eye evil because I am good?" (Mt. 20.)

When Christ told the parable of the laborers in the vineyard He taught, with wondrous clarity, the lesson, "Don't interfere!" He shows the owner of the vineyard paying workers, who had only worked for one hour, a full day's pay. This action, which he was entitled to take, incensed the workers who had "borne the burden of the day and the heats." They interfered; they complained. But they were snubbed! "Friends," said the owner. "I do you no wrong. Did you not agree with me for a penny? Take what is thine and go thy way!"

Even when we see others neglecting their duty, or quarreling, we are not thereby entitled to "lay down the law." "Sweep away the snow from thine own door," say the Chinese, "and heed not the frost upon thy neighbor's tiles." There are people who are forever telling others what to do and how to do it. They tell farmers what to plant and when; they tell parents what to give their children to eat and what clothes they should wear; they tell people who like to smoke that they should give up smoking; and they persuade their coffee-drinking friends to change over to tea. It never occurs to such people that Christ *meant* what He said: "Is it not lawful for me to do what I will?"

When, *as it appears to us,* other people are doing wrong, fighting for example, should we interfere? While it is possible to picture a case — that of a weakling being beaten to death in a lonely spot — where interference is justified, it still remains as a general rule that interference is wrong. "In every country dogs bite." One may, if he thinks it advisable, call the police, but charity demands no more. It is a wise adage that says: "Better pull a dog by the ears than interfere in a quarrel."

The lesson: "Don't interfere!" is not as well observed by us Americans, either as individuals or as a nation, as other lessons of democracy. We are prone to "poke our noses" into matters that do not concern us. We take it upon ourselves "to do the thinking" for other people, and to tell them how to manage their affairs.

In respect of Spain, to take one example, we have thought it right to tell this ancient, noble people how they should rule themselves, and how they should serve God. Because we find the two-party system of democracy "a going concern" among ourselves, we tell them to follow our system. Why do we not "keep what is ours and go our way" (Mt. 20), instead of acting as we do? The Spanish, though used to an autocratic or semiautocratic type of rule, have always known where and how to curb the supreme power. Theirs is the immortal adage: *"El rey va hasta do puede y no hasta do quiere"* — The king goes as far as he may, not as far as he would.

So far we have dealt almost exclusively with fair play in respect of the material rights of others. But what of their spiritual rights? Must they not also be regarded as sacred? Is he honorable who stands between men and their Maker, seeking to keep the creature from loving and serving his Creator? Is the teacher in a college acting honorably when he tries to undermine the faith and religion of students who are assembled to hear him discuss matters other than religion?

Christ said: "Suffer little children to come unto me!" The soul-snatcher, protected by his rostrum, dares to advise to the contrary, dropping the sneering hint that "religion is superstition." He is not only an interfering busybody, but he is a thief, who takes from others what is most precious to them by the mean trick of sophistry. "The Devil is subtle but he weaves a coarse web!"

It is not the way of honor and nobility, it is not fair play, to mislead or harm the hearts and souls of others. If we give, let us give good bread and not stones, edible fish and not serpents.

To "play it fair" in life is well within our power if we have good will and love honor. Genius is not needed. "For the honest man half his wits is enough — the whole is too little for a knave."

IV

KEEP WITHIN BOUNDS!

SOME things taste like more. We take more. Desire continues: we still want more. We take another. When will we stop?

We do not want to stop. Pleasure beckons. Happiness seems to be within reach. We tell ourselves: "Just another: then I'll be satisfied!" But satisfaction is elusive. Full content *always* evades our grasp! "Nothing," say the Arabs, "but a handful of dust will fill the eye of man!"

That passion should increase, and throw out new branches, is not entirely our fault. It is the way of nature. *"Mauvaise herbe croit toujours"* — Ill weeds grow apace. Our part is to keep our shears sharp and ready for use.

The box of candy from which we take another and another piece; the bottle of "bubble" from which we refill our glass; the car we drive ever faster and faster! Up to a certain point the candy, or the bottle, or the car is our friend, but after that point is passed it becomes our enemy. "If we give more to the flesh than we ought," wrote St.

Gregory, "we nourish an enemy." How prone we are to build up a monster that will destroy us!

The doctrine of moderation, "excellent moderation" as Montaigne called it from the Greek (μέτρον ἄριστον), the Stoic teaching of "just measure" (*via media*) is both wise and fascinating. It is based upon profound knowledge of human nature. Among other things it tells that "temperance is the best physic."

"There is a measure in all things," sang the poet Horace, "a certain limit, beyond or short of which right cannot be found." But what is that measure and where does it lie? The answer is not always easy to determine. We need to think earnestly, to "use our heads" to discover it:

> To find *the medium*, asks some share of wit
> And therefore 'tis a mark fools never hit (Cowper).

The word *temperance* comes from the Latin *temperare*, which means "to mingle in due proportions," "to qualify." Temperance is the virtue "which bridles concupiscence or which controls the yearning for pleasures and delights which most powerfully attract the human heart." It is defined also as "the righteous habit which makes a man govern his natural appetite for pleasures of the senses in accordance with the norm prescribed by reason." But these definitions appear to be too narrow. Temperance has to do not only with the senses but also with emotions, ideas, interests. There are intemperate emotions, ideas, and interests as well as appetites.

To find and hold the *via media* in every phase of our

conduct, to adhere to the principle of moderation in all things, one has to exercise restraint and cultivate frugality. One needs "a bridle of gold" to keep mind and body in check. To pull on that bridle when excitement and passion run riot requires guts. It means cutting off the gas that makes the engine race. "If thou wouldst quench the fire take off the fuel," says a proverb. Without courage and firmness temperance is impossible, and for courage and firmness we must go to God in prayer. Without Him we can do nothing.

In this country the word *temperance* has been more or less captured by the "antialcoholists." With no evil intent they have distorted the true meaning of the word. They call *total abstention* "temperance," whereas such an extreme measure is anything at all but temperance. No doubt total abstention is entirely necessary for those who cannot "touch the stuff" without losing their heads. No doubt, also, "more are drowned in the beaker than in the ocean," but the truth remains that temperance implies *moderation* and no more than that.

Antialcoholists also are in error in restricting the scope of temperance to the one habit of drinking. Temperance has to do equally with all our habits, those of eating, playing, smoking, gambling, money-making, as well as drinking. And when temperance in drinking or in any other habit is advocated, it is with temperance rather than fanaticism that the good cause should be pleaded. How often temperance advocates belie the very virtue that they preach, when:

Fire in each eye, and paper in each hand,
They rave, recite and madden through the land!
(Alex. Pope.)

It remains, however, that excessive drinking is one of our national calamities. Often we drink "to drown care," but as Benjamin Franklin wrote: "Drink does not drown care but waters it and makes it grow faster." Our difficulty lies in not "stopping" when we have had enough, or better still, a little before that point is reached. "The smaller the drink; the clearer the head; the cooler the blood," wrote William Penn. One should stop drinking before the head is fuddled and the blood heated. One should drink slowly, without greed, without excitement, taking a long time over one's first glass: postponing a "refill" as long as possible, or evading it. Even though others guzzle their wine or beer hoggishly one should keep cool and "take it easy." With great delicacy the French poet Alfred Musset reveals the manner of moderation:

Mon verre n'est pas grand,
Mais je bois dans mon verre.
(The glass I use is small and only from it do I drink.)

The correct mentality of the temperate man, his attitude of frugality, of refraining from taking (or possessing) overmuch, is well brought out by the question Socrates was wont to ask himself: *"How many things can I do without?"* Socrates knew, as every temperate man knows, that one is better off for taking less rather than more. We do not render ourselves poor by such conduct. "He is not poor who has enough for his needs" (Horace). Poverty is measured, not by what one possesses, but by what one desires. "He is not poor that hath little but he that desireth more." When, instead of doing without, we indulge ourselves to excess, we harm ourselves and we disgust others. There is little to admire in a glutton. "He that is full, is dull" (*Voll, toll*). That most attractive characteristic of manhood, self-control, disappears when one breaks out of bounds. On the other hand, to be content with a little, is to behave with grace and charm:

> What and how great, the virtue and the art,
> To live on little with a cheerful heart (Alex. Pope).

The doctrine of frugality, that the poet Pope expounds, is taught with magnificent power by St. Paul in a letter to his dearest friend, Bishop Timothy of Ephesus (1 Tim. 6).

Paul was not narrow or straight-laced about the use of God's gifts. He told Timothy: "Do not still drink water, but use a little wine for thy stomach's sake, and thy frequent infirmities." He was human in his dealings and in his ways, setting his friendships at a high price, and craving for his old cloak and his manuscripts, when the cold of winter assailed him in his Roman prison. But he put a high ideal of frugality before himself and us: "Having food and wherewith to be covered, with these we are content." He found "great gain" in being satisfied with the things God gave him; his slogan was "Godliness with contentment." Though he lived "in hunger and thirst, in fastings often, in cold and nakedness" (2 Cor.), his joyous mind never lost its equanimity. In tribulation he was never "distressed."

Paul's sharpest lesson on temperance, however, has to do with the inordinate desire of money. He warned that such greed for gold entangled men "in many sorrows" and brought "destruction and perdition" on them. Did he not teach, thereby, that "love of gold" is even more dangerous than "love of alcohol" and most of all requires the "gold bridle" of temperance to control it?

Paul invited us to see that gold has, at best, a transient value. "We brought nothing (no gold) into this world," he wrote, "and certainly we shall carry nothing (no gold) out." How pungent is the comment on these words that we find in the Italian proverb: *"L'ultimo vestito ce lo fanno senza tasche"* — Our last robe is made without pockets!

In our country the symbol of intemperance is not so much the saloon as "the exchange." There the passion to gain more and more is unbridled; in money-making "excellent moderation" and "just measure" are all but unknown virtues. The weed of greed grows unchecked; "the disposition of mind which sets bounds to the passions" is forgotten. Only when disaster strikes, when crashes come, is insensate fury checked. Then those "not ruled by the rudder are ruled by the rocks." Too late they see that there is wisdom as well as virtue in moderation; too late they recall Paul's warning that their greed would "entangle them in many sorrows."

The plain good sense of moderation is shown in a pretty line from Racine: *"Qui veut voyager loin ménage sa monture"* — He who would travel far should spare his steed. If we allow our horse to go "full pelt" from our doorstep, it is inevitable that he will collapse before our journey's done. Only a madman would ride in such fashion. Our saying "Easy does it!" contains the philosophy of temperance: "fast and furious" implies the "philosophy" of excess.

Where are we to find a man of real restraint? He does not work or walk or talk too fast or too slow; he does not say too much or too little. He knows that "He who speaks without care shall remember with sorrow," and he measures well his words. He is not changeful and restless but composed. He is not overdemonstrative toward friends, nor is he cold and aloof toward strangers. He is purposeful without being an insistent go-getter. He avoids pushing, shouting, and bustling around. His manner is quiet without being somber. He is neither an optimist nor a pessimist nor a loud-mouthed enthusiast. In all things he is evenminded and moderate; always he is sincere. What he has to do he does willingly, and with a light heart. When he can he rests, content at home, where "He hangs his plough-beam over the hearth" (Hesiod).

This kind of man, the man of restraint, the man who "keeps within bounds" is not a common American type. Here our motto is not, *"Ne quid nimis"* — Don't overdo anything! — rather is our motto: "Overshoes! Overboots!" which is to be interpreted as: "Wade in farther and farther!" It is excitement, not evenmindedness, that plays the largest role in our business and social life.

When anything has to be "put over" or displayed or sold the first step we take is "to work up interest" in our project, which in effect means to stir up noise and excitement. The help of verbal and literary "barkers" is invoked. Radio and television are called on to lend a hand. The drumming continues until a state of near-hysteria is induced. The fact that excitement is neurotic and unhealthy; the fact that it prevents good thinking and calm judgment is disregarded. In order to sell a car, to select a beauty queen, to win a football game, to elect a member to Congress, there must be fanfare, tumult, and an orgy of emotion. To get something done, to collect dimes to combat polio, or to persuade citizens to lend their services to civil defense, there must be mad clamor that reduces the freedom of the individual to its psychological minimum.

It is not enough for us that a thing be gigantic and colossal. Unless we are assured that it is "supercolossal" we remain unimpressed. Our jaded attention is not attracted unless headlines scream the news at us. Our wearied imaginations remain unmoved unless gruesome, tragic pictures are thrust before our eyes. Behind the pictures we must hear sobs and lurid whispers. No quiet news appraisal, that keeps close to the facts, is tolerable any longer; we crave for distortions even though we know from experience that denials and contradictions are slated soon to follow. Our sound and healthy taste for temperate words and temperate thoughts — for moderation — is lost. Now we find ourselves addicts of the dread and deadly drug, *excitement!*

In what direction can we look for escape from the frenzy of mind and manners that our social environment induces? How are we to free ourselves from the wild whirl that engulfs us? Is there no retreat to which we can make our way, there to find a little contentment and repose? Christ knew the need humans feel for quiet. Once He said to His disciples: "Come ye apart into a desert place and rest a little!"

For many of us the "desert place" where we can find rest is the virtue of self-control, frugality, moderation. In temperance we can find freedom from what harasses us most of all, namely, our insistent desires. In this "desert place" a certain *poverty* awaits us, but "Poverty," as Lucan taught, "is the mother of manhood." It takes effort "to do without things," to do with less smokes, less drinks, less visits to the movies and the ball games. Temperance insists on "a little less of those things you crave for." Even as regards food, we have to exercise spiritual economy. "He who really wants to save," says a Danish proverb, "must begin with his mouth!" Honor is a high vocation. It calls for many a sacrifice!

When Horace sang, as quoted above: "There is a measure *in all things,* a certain limit, beyond or short of which right cannot be found," he laid down a principle of universal application, one that should tone down the ardor of faddists, hobby chasers, and "extremists" of all kinds.

Horace knew that people are prone to become obsessed with one aim or idea and to spend their lives in its pursuit to the exclusion of all else. There are people who have no interest outside stamps or football or antiques or hunting or watching birds or growing orchids. Their overspecialization is intemperate. They cage themselves within a narrow space like hermits. They are Stylites without the religious motive he had for his behavior.

While a hobby is good as a means of culture, recreation, or profit, there is not enough in any one hobby to feed a man's soul so that he may live like a brother among brothers. An all-absorbing hobby cuts us off from others: "One man, no man" (εἶς ἀνὲρ, οὐδέις ἀνὲρ), the Greeks said. One ceases to be a man when he cuts himself off from men! Our aim should be to enlarge the scope of our lives, to cultivate many interests.

A temperate man, though he enjoys fishing more than anything else, will still have time to do a bit of gardening, to go once in a while to the football stadium, to read good books, to watch the stars that reveal the goodness and eternal splendor of God. He will seek out the mysteries and charms of nature and art, and resist the enslavement that one particular fascination exercises. He is temperate because he is universal; he runs and leaps and dances as well as stands, rod in hand, while the river flows by. He knows that "thought is the measure of life" and that life will remain unknown to him, unless he approach it through many channels.

Temperance and self-control are, of course, the purpose

of Christian asceticism. Self-denial is involved, without which "we all perish." The lesson may seem hard but it is necessary. To save our lives, as Christ taught us, we must be prepared to lose them.

Temperance, as we look at it, is a fight against self. But what of the intemperance in which we indulge? May it not also be looked at, with greater truth, as a fight against self?

In what is called *Papyrus Prisse,* the oldest book in the world, dating back three and a half thousand years before Christ, we find among the precepts of Ptah-hotep the inverted doctrine of temperance as I have stated it above: *"He that is wrong* (i.e., intemperate) *fights against himself."* It is no little comfort for us to know that the oldest and wisest thoughts and feelings of the human race are all on the side of temperance.

Temperance is so necessary in social life, in life in all its phases, that without it honorable conduct is impossible. Unless "we keep within bounds" we hurt and injure our neighbors; we offend against their souls as well as their bodies; we rob them of spiritual as well as material goods.

To a brave and honorable man an occasional act of self-restraint and sacrifice, an occasional loss of pleasure and self-indulgence is not by any means unbearable. Instead of pitying himself he smiles bravely — he sees the good that results — and he is proudly content. His it is to say, with the color and humor of our oldest philosophy: "I have lost the ring, yet the fingers are still there!"

CHAPTER

V

NEVER PANIC!

WE ARE all liable to panic and "go to pieces" if we allow
fear to possess us. The occasion may be relatively unimportant. The radio announces a sharp drop on the stock
exchange; our doctor looks grave as he takes our blood
pressure; it is night, and someone dear to us is a few
hours overdue; we notice smoke curling upward as we sit
in a crowded auditorium; whatever the occasion, if we
panic we will act like fools or madmen. We should always
look calamity in the face with calm. As the Spaniards say:
"When you see your house in flames, approach and warm
yourself by it."

The best of us may panic. On the lake a boatload of
seasoned and sturdy fishermen, frightened by rising winds
and waves, gave way to panic and awakened from slumber
their Master who needed to sleep. He asked them why
they had acted so. Panic never does any good — always
it runs counter to honor!

The fear that drives us to panic arises from the antici-
pation of some loss or suffering. It is, as it were, a fore-

taste of pain. But to taste pain, in advance, should not change a man from reason to unreason. In life, suffering and loss have to be met and borne. As pleasure is not the highest good, pain is not the ultimate ill. Cicero associated and contrasted temperance and courage when he wrote: "No man can be temperate who considers pleasure the highest good, nor brave if he considers pain the greatest evil." Courage is grounded in right reason as well as in an honest heart.

The man who can "take it," who can face calamity without being unduly upset, who is mindful of others when shadows close in on him, has the essential element of fortitude. He takes the measure of suffering, whether mental or physical, and sees its boundaries. When duty calls he cleaves to it though it burn his hands. He has the wisdom to accept good things and things that hurt alike from God's hands and to thank God for them. "I am ready, O Lord," says À Kempis, "to accept from Your hand both good and evil alike, the sweet and bitter together, sorrow with joy; and for all that happens to me, I am grateful." A brave man does not run away in panic when trouble overtakes him. Only the man who is without courage runs away. As the proverb goes: "He who has not courage should have legs!"

Before we proceed with our discussion of courage, we take note of the undeniable fact that mankind *despises,* and has always despised, cowardice. While the imprudent man is laughed at, the unjust man avoided or hated, the intemperate man disliked (or perhaps pitied), the cowardly man is contemned! He is more foolish than the imprudent man, more cruel than the unjust man, and more unbridled than the intemperate man. At times his cowardice makes him a selfish beast who tramples on the bodies of women and children in the fury of his escape from danger. The coward becomes the arch egotist, the sadist, the thief. There is no crime that the coward will not commit when panic seizes him. He is a danger to everyone, the enemy of everyone; he claws and bites everyone. Though often pictured as "the sheep whom the wolves devour," *the coward is a potential wolf himself.* His existence serves one purpose, however; it serves to prove to us convincingly that courage is not merely a becoming virtue that we should seek to have, but a virtue that it is absolutely necessary for us to have, if we are to live decent, honorable lives.

It is customary, when discussing courage, to distinguish between physical and moral courage. The distinction, which is easy to make, does not go very deep. Both kinds of courage are fundamentally the same. It is due to the fact that the Greeks threw the spotlight on war, when they exemplified bravery, that the epithet "hero" in much of literature denotes a valiant soldier. "Fortitude," wrote Aristotle, "is the virtue of a man, who being confronted with a noble occasion of encountering the danger of death, meets it fearlessly." The ideal of the brave man, to wit the soldier-hero, was to die for his country.

From Aristotle's line of thinking we turn to that of the wise and peaceable À Kempis. For him courage meant the facing of adversity. "We know not often what we are able to do, but temptation shows us *what we are. . . .* They that cannot bear temptation become reprobate and fall away." Those who are brave survive and grow greater for their fidelity. "Adversity makes men!" Though by no means an ascete, Robert Ingersoll held the same view as À Kempis. He said: "The greatest test of courage on earth is to bear defeat without losing heart."

Among the ancients the question arose: "Is there more courage shown in attack than in defense?" Aquinas held strongly to the opinion that "the principal act of courage is to hold out, to stand firm against dangers, rather than to make an assault." Perhaps one should leave it to the modern soldier to decide this question with finality. He would know whether it is harder to remain in one's fox-hole under heavy bombardment, than to fix bayonet and charge across a bullet-swept field. To make such a charge would not have been possible or desirable to Aquinas. Only "to stand firm" would have been within his physical power.

In modern times due notice is taken of the courage that is displayed in avocations of peace. The gallant doctor who fights an epidemic, the scientist who pursues a research in spite of poverty and fatigue, the social worker who labors in obscurity to better the conditions of the underprivileged — all are hailed as "heroes" today, and we have a better understanding of Shakespeare's words:

> He is truly valiant who can wisely suffer
> The worst that man can breathe.

Not all of us are called upon to fight physical enemies, but there is no one among us but has to fight spiritual battles, and we know how trying they can be and how much courage they call for. In a spiritual battle the foe is invisible, intangible, elusive. We cannot see him, or grab him by the throat. He does not observe "Queensbury rules," nor does he observe any time limit, stopping at the sound of a bell. A spiritual fight is against weariness, discouragement, darkness. The enemy penetrates our defenses and fights us within as well as without. He plays on our feelings, our imaginings, our fears. "Where the devil cannot come he sends." And the fight is deadly because the stake is the highest — our immortal soul. Peace is simulated; then the attack is renewed suddenly and treacherously. Who can deny that real courage (we call it *desperate courage*) is needed in fighting temptation?

In respect of courage there is one thing that we should never do, that is to boast that it is ours. We may hear a tale of cowardice and be inclined to brag: "I would have acted otherwise!" Let us not forget Aesop's words: "It is easy to be brave from a safe distance." There are many Falstaffs among us who tell us of the brave things that they intend to perform. As in the case of Falstaff, "The worst wheel of the cart makes the most noise." How can we tell how we shall feel, much less what our reaction will be, when we come face to face with real danger? Wrote La Rochefoucauld: "No man can answer for his courage who has never been in danger."

Many of us, as well as being "lions at home" before we go out to take part in some contest, remain "lions" (in our own esteem) when we return again and tell of our feats of gallantry. As our tale unfolds we lay claim to great achievements. " 'We hounds killed the hare!' quoth the lap-dog!"

What are the characteristics of courage? By what marks is true courage known?

First of all, courage has to be *distinguished from rashness:* it is based in reason and has in it a due admixture of prudence. When there is no proportion between the end and the means, when a pygmy attacks a giant, we have rashness, not courage. "Courage," wrote Emerson, "consists in equality to the problem before us." It is not an explosion of passion or folly or force; it sees, thinks, reckons. "Courage ought to have eyes as well as arms." It does not throw away the yardstick of moderation; there is temperance as well as prudence in it.

The college boy who on a dare attempts to scale a perilous mountain peak, without adequate safeguards, or to swallow an overdose of sleeping pills to show that he is not afraid, does not display true courage. Acts divorced from good sense and reason have no virtue in them, and do not belong among acts of courage.

A second characteristic of courage is that *it faces danger and suffering.* Its glance is steady and searching. It appraises the strength of the foe. It remains cool and does not give way to excitement or any other emotion. When Alexander the Great was warned that an immense horde of Persians was marching against his small force, he said: "One butcher does not fear many sheep!"

A brave man does not panic *because he does not over-estimate the danger that confronts him.* He knows that threats and dangers are liable to seem greater than they really are. He knows that "a wild boar is often held by a small dog," and that "Fortune favors the brave." The steadiness of a leader inspires others and arouses their hopes. "What a new face courage puts on everything!"

Another mark of true courage is its *pertinacity.* It perseveres, without wavering. "No surrender . . . not an inch," is its cry. Courage endures when it is true and sincere; it holds out to the end. Compromise is often a sign of failing courage; though, of course, it can also be a sign of justice and wisdom. But when a cause is un-equivocally right, there should be "no backward step."

A brave man "hangs on" and refuses to admit failure. "Where one door shuts another opens." He tries this means and that of reaching his goal. His perseverance is often crowned with victory. "Leg over leg the dog reached Dover," as the saying goes.

True courage calls for *faith,* for the confidence that faith in God inspires. A man confronted by suffering and difficulties knows that only from God can adequate aid come. He knows too that "whom God will aid no man can hurt." He finds his courage grows when he places his confidence in God.

To Americans, whose national motto is "In God We Trust," it comes natural to build up our courage and our confidence in this divine trust. The Prophet Jeremiah (17:5–10) tells us what this means in a moving picture: "Blessed be the man that trusted in the Lord, and the Lord shall be his confidence. And he shall be as a tree that is planted by the waters, that spreadeth out its roots towards the moisture; and it shall not fear when the heat cometh. And the leaf thereof shall be green, and in the time of drought it shall not be solicitous, neither shall it cease at any time to bring forth fruit."

Though things grow darker and darker, the faith of a brave man does not fail. He sees in the climax of evil, the vigil of better times. He knows, as the Persians say, that "when the defile is narrowest it begins to open out." And he is not afraid to take risks that are reasonable and necessary. He knows, as does the fisherman, that "he who would catch fish must venture his bait." With confidence comes a certain *élan,* a vivacity, that is optimistic in tone. When reason dictates that a fence *has* to be crossed, in spite of the danger involved, the man of courage does not hesitate. "It is the best dog that leaps the stile first!"

It would be false to think that courage is purely spiritual and wholly independent of our physical make-up. The "animal rage" that is latent in us (and that is taken into account by Aquinas) is founded in part in our physical nature. Father Rickaby, S.J., remarking on the dual quality of fortitude, writes: "There is much interaction between moral and physical qualities and our duty is to cultivate the two departments of fortitude conjointly" (*Catholic Encyclopedia,* "Courage"). He indicates that the physical conditions conducive to courage are good health, buoyant spirits, and experience of shocks, for instance, "battle noises." On the other hand, ill-health, lassitude, and melancholia militate against courage. The man who is weak from hunger, or suffering from a toothache, is, *per se,* less likely to act heroically than a well-fed man with perfect denture! Our courage is, thus, to some extent dependent on "how we feel."

Our courage is also dependent on the thoughts that occupy our minds at the time of a crisis. "As a man thinketh in his heart," says Holy Scripture, "so is he." We know that thought is "the seed of action," though it is the will that carries the thought into effect. If a man allows himself to be obsessed with the idea of failure and defeat, he diminishes his courage. In facing difficulty we have to nourish the thought of success, to "autosuggest" ourselves, if necessary, into a happy frame of mind, repeating to ourselves along the lines of M. Coué: "I know I can . . . I know I can!" The boy who whistles a brave air, "to keep up his courage," as he goes alone through a dark wood, is a good psychologist.

It is the imagination that is the worst foe of courage. The imagination is prone to present a thousand and one unreal dangers and difficulties before our minds. It awakens fears and puts upon us the terrible burden of fighting fear. "Wake not at every dog's bark," we are told. But does not a slight noise at night alarm some of us? If we have had trouble in the past, connected with some night noise, our fears are all the worse. The Hebrew proverb reminds us that "one bitten by a serpent is afraid of a rope end."

It is the part of a brave man to do his duty in spite of fear. Often, however great his courage, he is unable to drive away fear; his teeth may chatter, and his limbs tremble.

> The brave man is not he who *feels* no fear,
> For that were stupid and irrational.
> But he whose noble soul its fear subdues,
> And bravely dares the danger! (Joanna Baillie.)

It is not cowards only who "die many times before their deaths." Courageous men, of vivid imagination, often see the signal light of death without faltering. As the Chinese say: "The hero does not ask if there be evil omens; he views death as going home."

Though courage is primarily a virtue of the individual, there is also a communal virtue of courage: the courage of an army as a whole, or of a people as a whole. It is spoken of as *morale* — the morale of an army or the morale of a nation. As a result of spreading excitement or emotion, this morale is said to rise or to fall. Victory enhances morale; defeat lowers it. A great calamity may induce hysterical fear.

In recent times the instrument of "threat" has been used to lower other nations' morale and to induce cowardice. A threat is only effective when it succeeds in awakening cowardice in the other party. But what lies behind a threat? How is a threat to be interpreted?

Whether or not the ancients were right about it, they

interpreted a threat as a sign of fear and of weakness in the party that threatens. "Dogs that bark at a distance never bite," they said. There is another ancient saying still stronger and more definite to the same effect. In French it reads: *"Tel menace qui a grand peur"* — He who threatens is full of fear. In general it is wise to disregard threats, and to take heart, inasmuch as they reveal weakness in one's enemy.

"Never panic!" Never let fear control your behavior! Such is the fourth rule of honor.

This is an easier rule to observe than the rules of prudence, justice, and temperance. The average man or woman finds no insuperable difficulty in being brave because he and she find within the primitive, powerful stimulus of self-preservation.

If a man is humble, if he keeps within his own rights and respects the rights of others, he can "sit in his own place and no man can make him move."

It is not on account of the glamour that often goes with heroic conduct that courage belongs to honor but because courage is necessary in order to fulfill our obligations to others and to help them all we can. *The courageous man is swift and sure in action.* When his brother needs assistance he does not refuse through fear of difficulty; he gives it without delay. He knows that: "Slow help is no help."

The more love there is in our hearts for God and for our fellow men, the easier courage will come; the less we shall be tempted to "throw up the sponge" and run away. St. John's words obtain: "Love drives out fear!"

CHAPTER

VI

DO YOUR JOB!

À KEMPIS asks the pertinent question: "Why seekest thou
rest, since thou art born to labor?" With humor the Spanish peasant demands: "Where wilt thou go, Ox, that thou
wilt not have to plough?" The questions are fundamentally
the same.

Who can hope to escape the burden of toil? Who can
doubt man's obligation to work? In the hard facts of life
the Divine Will proclaims loud and clear: "Man must
labor!"

But labor is not just labor and no more; work is not
just work! The man who accepts the divine decree and
submits to it, worships as he toils. St. Benedict condensed
this truth in three words: "Labor is prayer."

The pagan philosopher Seneca wrote, forestalling the
Christian teaching of St. Benedict: "It is unbecoming (dishonorable) in man to fear to sweat." He is a coward who
despises his job or fails to do it as best he can! He is a

fool who thinks he can live and do nothing. "Even the ripest fruit does not drop into one's mouth!"

In one of his fables La Fontaine remarks: "By the work one knows the workman." The worker reveals himself in his work; he not only shows what talent he possesses, but also his moral quality. He writes his ability and his character into what he does. Has he skill and art? Does he reach out toward an ideal? Is his outlook on life serious? Has he a sense of duty and of honor? You can tell all when you study his work.

It is rare to come upon a piece of work that is really well done — and *finished* — as it should be. These are days of fast, careless, slipshod work. "Honest labor has a lovely face," someone wrote. It is not often that we behold that beauty!

How important is it that work should be done well and carefully?

It takes but a moment to realize that our well-being and our safety, as well as our peace of mind, are dependent upon the kind of work that is done for us. If the electrician we employ to wire our house does an inefficient job, we may be burned to death or ruined by a fire. A clumsy pharmacist may poison us. A cook can send a whole family to bed with agonizing cramps. We hear of submarines failing to rise to the surface; of planes loaded with passengers crashing; of automobiles "out of control" smashing into one another and killing the passengers. Drivers and pilots are not always to blame for mishaps. *As often as not it is the ill-made or ill-designed machine, put together by careless hands, that is the cause of tragedy.*

Most of us have a goal of one kind or another in life, some status or some reward to which we would attain. "To arrive" we must work, with our minds and with our hands. "He who would eat the kernel must crack the shell" (Plautus). Some, no doubt, seem to attain their ambition swiftly and easily, as it were by chance, but the vast majority of men discover that "life gives nothing to men unless they work hard." Work is the price we have to pay, and unless the work is good it will not for long pass currency. Edison taught a self-evident truth when he said, "There is no substitute for hard work!"

A job gives us, first of all, the chance to find ourselves. The job, whatever it is, presents a new and different experience, one that provokes unfamiliar efforts and unfamiliar thoughts. Ideas are born. They may lead the way to new opportunities. "All work," wrote Carlyle, "is as seed sown. It grows and spreads and sows itself anew." To put it very simply, "one thing leads to another." A *chance* is likely to present itself somewhere in between. On the other hand, if we do no work, if we take no job, we remain in the dark about ourselves, and we are not accosted by opportunity.

The hard worker, like the office boy in the Admiralty long ago, who "polished so well the handle of the big front door," makes an impression on someone or other, and finally makes his way upward. Things seem to happen that way in life. Work counts and is counted. Success follows and then, perchance, fame. But whether success and fame be ours or not, whether or not material benefits be our reward for hard work, we please and serve God and win His love, by honest, faithful toil.

When we hire ourselves to do a job, are we, or are we not, supposed to put the best we have into doing the job right? Is there, latent in our contract, that understanding? Are we supposed "to throw our whole souls" into the job?

When a young man, I worked for a highly respectable and old-fashioned firm as an office clerk. The work I was given to do was uninteresting, and I considered it "beneath me." I had had a classical education and *I felt myself superior to mere bookkeeping.*

When the end of the year came around, the board of directors of the firm interviewed each member of the staff. When my turn to be interviewed came, I found myself sitting at the end of a long mahogany table, at the sides of which sat directors. Facing me, at the head of the table, sat the managing director, a tall, grave man, who wore *pince-nez.*

For a while he looked at me and then, mentioning my name, he asked: "Do you throw your whole soul into your work?" Evidently, he had received none too flattering reports about me.

I didn't know what to answer. I sought refuge in an evasion, and I felt very ashamed!

It had never occurred to me that I could or should "throw my whole soul" into keeping books. My work, I know, was far from neat. I presume it was often inaccurate. What I was being paid to do, what I had contracted to do, I was not doing! What then was I but a thief?

In those days I grumbled over my job. And, like all who grumble about their work, I was in no mood to do good work. I guess I lowered the morale of others in my office. It was a good admonition that the beloved Uncle Remus gave to the cow that was groaning as it pulled the yoke for him. "You do de pullin', Sis Cow, en I'll do de gruntin'!"

It is interesting to dwell for a moment on man's capacity for "vicarious labor." Man has a mysterious instinct to occupy himself in observing the work of others. What crowds watch when a job is afoot near the sidewalk! We look on, absorbed, as other men dig or hammer. If we understand what is being done we are prone to criticize. "The man on the dyke always hurls well!" as the Irish say. If there be a worker "draped over his shovel," taking a little time off, we watch him with interest. When will he start in again, we ask? Our vicarious toil does not tire us. "The burden is light on the shoulders of another." It is for enjoyment that we look on, not in order to lend the toilers a hand. There is fascination in watching others work; let us hope that our nature makes us in this way pay an unconscious tribute to labor.

When we have a job to do, when we hire out to do a job, it is wrong to waste time in beginning, seeking, as it were, a way of escape. The job may look tedious, uninviting, but that is no justification for hesitating and "dawdling." *The pertinent thing is that it is our job, and that it is our duty to do it well.* We should take up our tools at once and go at it knowing that "the best way out is always through." Also, it is good to keep in mind that: "The morning hour has gold in its mouth."

St. Paul had little sympathy with slackers. He wrote to the Thessalonians: "If a man will not work, neither let him eat!" St. Paul "labored more abundantly" than anyone. Rather than be a burden to others, he worked with his hands. He gloried in work for he knew that "a workman need not be ashamed." The stamp of perfection was on his output. We recognize the fullness and beauty of a master's work in Paul's epistles and letters. All he touched he adorned!

Men and women who shirk work bring various misfortunes on themselves. The maladies and miseries of life fall heaviest on them. For such, wrote Carlyle, there is but one cure. "Work is a grand cure for all the maladies and miseries that beset mankind." People grow sick in mind and in body because of idleness. They crave for sympathy in their self-caused distress, but they deserve none. *"The sick one,"* wrote Montaigne caustically, *"is not to be pitied who has the means of cure up his sleeve."*

Some who read these pages will exclaim, "None of that applies to me! I have too much to do! I do more than my share!"

There are those who forget the principle "first things first." What should come first with them is the work they are contracted (or ordered) to do. Instead of being satisfied to do that work, they assume other tasks. They do wrong in attempting to carry, or in pretending that they can carry, a double load. To attempt to accomplish too much results in accomplishing nothing. "Dogs that put up many hares kill none." There is no honor or justice in deceiving others (or ourselves) as to the quantity or quality of the work we can do. If we really have "too much to do" we should get out from under that burden.

Living, as I have lived for years, in an old ranch house in California, I have had varied experience with men who undertook to do jobs for me, from carpenters to farriers and chimney sweepers! I've had, like others, many a harassing disappointment in the quality of the work done, or in the failure to do what was promised. On the Aran Isles, I had seen a woman of ninety years up on her cottage roof mending the thatch, but the chimney sweeper I employed, although a member of the local fire brigade, was afraid to get up on my little chimney.

An expert who constructed an arbor would have seen it in a heap a few weeks later had he come back to admire his work. A slight breeze had knocked it over! The farrier I engaged to shoe a mare gave up his attempt to shoe her hind hoofs. She wasn't tame enough for him!

Side by side with disappointing work, I've seen the amazing grandeur of honest and spirited work.

In a storm, a huge oak tree fell across my only avenue, blocking it completely. It was a stunning "disaster" and, it seemed to me, almost irremediable. "No road up to the sky: no door into the ground."

After a phone call, an elderly Italian and his son arrived with saws, axes, and some hand tackle. It was still early when they went to work. Together they sawed through the great trunk at one place after another. They chopped off big branches with their axes. Often they were in serious danger but they kept alert. When the sawing was finished they began with the tackle. The immense stump was pulled out. Big limbs were hauled to one side. When darkness fell the avenue was cleared.

These two men, one old and one young, had faced a terrific job with quiet courage, carrying it to completion with skill and will power. In such a job there was real work — and more than work — there was moral achievement. "Nothing is difficult to a well-willed man."

Earlier in this chapter I quoted the saying: "Honest labor has a lovely face!" Certainly Christ was enamoured of that face! How tenderly, how affectionately, He praised those watchmen and those stewards of His parables, who carried out efficiently the work that was given them to do! With what unforgettable words He addressed them: "Well done! Good and faithful servants!"

"No sweat: no sweet!" "No pains: no gains!" Practical wisdom, virtue, self-respect — all combine in endorsing as a necessary rule of honor the counsel: "Do your job!"

VII

PAY YOUR DEBTS!

DEBTS are so burdensome that there is much truth in the proverb: "He that gets out of debt grows rich!"

Debts have to be paid, and the sooner the better. While we are in debt others have power over our liberty; we are poor with the worst kind of poverty. "Owe no man anything!" said St. Paul and his advice is good. There is an excuse for people to go into debt for the necessaries of life, such as a house or a car; but only fools go into debt for items of luxury or convenience. "Better to go to bed supperless than to rise in debt!"

The debts against which St. Paul and the proverbs warn are debts of justice, and it is not with these that we are here concerned. There is another kind of debt to be discussed presently, debts of honor or, in other words, debts of love. For some of these debts we are not responsible; some of them we can never fully repay. There are debts of gratitude, for example, that surpass our will and our capacity ever to repay. There are debts incurred by promises that involve payments up until the last hours of life. There are debts due by way of amendment for wrongs that we have done, that we may not be able to meet. There is lastly the great long-lasting debt of love that we owe to all our fellow men, in acts of giving and serving. To this St. Paul referred in the second part of his famous advice: *"Owe no man anything but to love one another."*

First among the debts of honor come debts incurred when we promise to do something for another. Such a promise is a contract. It should be remembered; it should be fulfilled. It is like an I O U signed, if not by our hand, by our lips and heart.

Are we faithful or unfaithful? It is our fidelity that is at issue in a promise. Whether the promise be about a little or a big thing; whether made to one who is important or to one who does not count; whether it be about the writing of a letter or the payment of a considerable sum in cash; it is the same fidelity that is involved. As the lovable Uncle Remus said: "A promise is a promise dough you make it in de dark er de moon." Once made, a promise should haunt us until fulfilled. Though it be quite excusable, and even wise and right, to refuse to make a promise, once deliberately made (if the thing promised be honest), nothing can excuse the breaking of it.

People make light of their promises. They promise too hastily and too recklessly. They feel it easy and even pleasant to promise, for a promise costs nothing. "He is poor indeed," says a proverb, "who can promise nothing!" People promise so as to please, to win a grateful smile or a flattering word. They make so many promises that they run into debt. Then they renege! They allow promises to slip out of their memories. "Apt to promise; apt to forget." They fail to keep their word. Their honor is tarnished.

But there is something else hurt besides their honor. The promisee, the one for whose benefit we made the promise, is "let down," disappointed, and perhaps even betrayed. It is not the promiser, but the promisee, who is in a position to assess the value and importance of a promise. It is he who counted on something that he wanted, perhaps very badly. A broken promise can mean a broken heart. A broken promise humiliates and deceives. What kind of love does a broken promise indicate? It indicates no love at all, but forgetfulness, disregard, contempt!

We should never promise anything that is not well within our power to do or to give. We should make *few promises*, for promises are not easy to keep. We should take pains to remember our promises and they should be very definite. We should not promise when we are emotionally disturbed or excited, but only with a clear, calm mind. Our promise should be in simple words and sincere; said with a true purpose.

'Tis not the many oaths that make the truth,
But the plain single vow that is vowed true! (Shakespeare.)

When we make a promise to a child or a sick person or someone in need, it is doubly cruel on our part, and grossly lacking in honor, to fail to keep our word. The child will count very much on getting the toy promised him; the sick person will await the promised visit impatiently and tearfully. The poor man, to whom we have promised a job, will be crushed and embittered, if we default. "Promises are the pitfalls of fools," it is said, but we should make sure not to dig pitfalls for our brothers. The man who breaks his promises breaks himself. We cannot go on deceiving others with false words and pledges, without blunting our sense of honor. "Debts and lies are generally mixed together," said Rabelais; the excuses we make when we fail to fulfill our promises are usually falsehoods. *He alone is honorable of whom it can be said: "He always keeps his word!"*

The debt of honor that comes second to fidelity is gratitude. Gratitude is so admired and praised that the phrase "debt of gratitude" is accepted as indicating man's obligation in this respect. Seneca voiced a common belief when he wrote: "Nothing is more honorable than a grateful heart." Cicero called gratitude "the greatest virtue and the mother of all the rest," and he said, *"There is no quality I would rather have and be thought to have than gratitude."*

We know the sweetness of gratitude and the bitterness of ingratitude; we have felt a thrill when someone whom we helped came back to thank us and to tell us of his affection and his indebtedness; also, alas! we have felt

the chill, the freezing of the "wintry wind," when someone whom we helped repaid us with indifference and
contempt. We recognize the beauty and wisdom of Paul's
words: "in everything give thanks." The "boons unbought"
that God bestows on men, the "every best gift" that comes
down from above on just and unjust alike, force our minds
into seeing the necessity and the reasonableness of thank-
fulness to God. If the fear of God is the beginning of wisdom, thanking God is the first step of true virtue.

Gratitude is described as "the memory of the heart."
It does not consist merely of words — though words are
of use and helpful; *it consists in acts,* in doing, in the
efforts of the hand and the will to make due return for
benefits received. Gratitude, as Aesop wrote: "is the sign
of noble souls"; souls who grasp the truth of the adage,
"One good turn deserves another." Gratitude belongs
especially to those who have insight, who are humble,
for they are objective and sensitive to reality. "When they
drink from the stream they remember the spring." They
see indebtedness for what it is; they see how they are
and have been dependent upon others. Not to resent
such dependence is the foundation of gratitude.

Proud, resentful souls, who admit no indebtedness for
love and service, who take the help that others give them
as "their due," who take it as a matter of course that their
parents or friends should protect and cherish them, are
ungrateful. Their way is to accept everything and to hand
out nothing in exchange. There is no love in their hearts
and, as a consequence, they never really live.

The man may last, but never lives,
Who much receives but nothing gives (T. Gibbons).

That true gratitude consists *in doing something* to re-pay a favor is illustrated in the Gospel story of the man born blind (Jn. 9). This man received from Christ an unsolicited favor and he was deeply moved. He admitted before all what "the man that is called Christ" had done for him. When for a second time he was cross-questioned by the Pharisees, and when Christ's good name was impugned, he stood up bravely for Christ. He mocked at the proud and powerful Pharisees because they did not know "whence he is." He said: "Unless this man were of God he could not do anything!" He was punished for his loyalty and thrown out of the temple. But Christ found him again, and gave him another and greater gift. Christ loved gratitude.

There is no one of us but, looking back on life, can see someone who did us a favor or was kind to us. That kind act is deathless in our memory, but what have we done about it? Is our benefactor dead? If so, we can pray that his soul find rest and peace. Is he alive? If so, we can still do something to make him happy for an hour. The way of honor is not sentimental; it is realistic.

In addition to debts of honor in respect of our promises, and in respect of gratitude, we have debts incurred by the hurts we have inflicted on others. We owe amends, the righting of wrongs, the healing of wounds.

It is in good taste and reasonable to repent of injuries done to others, and to express sorrow for them. It is something even to say: "Gee! I'm sorry!" There is nobility in confessing to a fault and in trying to expiate it. Ages ago Homer wrote: "The hearts of good men admit of atonement." It is through atonement that forgiveness and renewed innocence are attained.

> Who after his transgressions does repent,
> Is half, or altogether, innocent (Herrick).

There are those who despise repentance as a weakness, who feel no shame for, but only pride in, their misdeeds. They are so besotted in their egotism that they know of no pain save such twinges as they themselves feel. The pain in others' hearts does not concern them, and they care not to move a hand to lessen or ease such pain. When they wrong others, when they insult or hurt them, they leave them to fester in their sores. Such is the philosophy of those who refuse to make amends.

When we do a wrong to another, and recognize it as such, it is well to ask forgiveness without delay. "*We all go astray,*" wrote Voltaire, very soberly, "*but the least imprudent is he who the earliest comes to repent.*" Though years have passed since we inflicted the injury, it is not too late to pay our debt of honor. "He comes never late who comes repentant." It is a fine achievement to secure forgiveness, to put an end to a hate, to convert an enemy into a friend.

Who can hope to live a life of honor, a life marked by respect for his fellow men, who is not always willing and ready both to forgive and to seek forgiveness?

We now reach the final debt which honor imposes on us. It is a deep-seated and long-lasting debt. It is our obligation to allow others, our brothers, to partake of the good things of which we are in possession. The purpose of honor is to be happy and to make others happy. "The hand that gives, gathers!" It gathers happiness.

At Clongowes Wood College (Ireland), the ancient and much respected "boarding" school where I was educated, there was a custom among the boys called "giving shares." It was an old custom, probably dating back a century or more. It was best illustrated in connection with special "feeds" (feasts) that were at various times given for groups of boys; prize winners in exams, captains and secretaries of divisions, curators of libraries, and so forth. On the eve of such feeds friends of the lucky boys about to participate would ask "Shares?" Then, when the feed was over, the boys who had sat down to a table laden with goodies would bring out "shares" to their friends, consisting of cakes, apples, and candy; sometimes half a leg of cold turkey!

The spirit of shares ramified in various directions. Boys who received hampers from home gave shares. Boys who were well supplied with cash and who could buy plenty of "shop" at the biweekly school store, gave shares to needy friends. It was considered mean, if your pocket contained candy, and you were sitting near another boy in the library, or out with him on a walk, not to share what you had with your companion. It belonged to our code of honor, as Clongowes boys, to give and receive in a free friendly way. Ours was the old Italian thought: "Friends tie their purses with cobweb's thread."

Many decades have passed since I gave or received "shares" at Clongowes, and they have left me more convinced than ever of the innate nobility of generosity. All things are meant for all; the words *thine* and *mine* have only relative meaning. What you do not need is in part for me; what I do not need, you have a claim to. *"Giving and keeping,"* wrote Cervantes, *"require brains."* The man "who uses his head" knows the need of giving as well as the need of moderation in keeping. He knows the meaning of the oft and variously expressed thought:

> The only things we ever keep,
> Are what we give away! (Ginsberg.)

No matter how much we do or how much we give to a person in need, no matter how lovingly we offer our alms, we should not look upon our good deed otherwise than as a poor effort to fulfill an obligation, to repay a debt.

It is honor which gives us this sixth rule: "Pay your debts!"

VIII

NEVER LIE!

THE search for facts, for knowledge, for truth, is characteristic of the times. The scientist who exemplifies pursuit of knowledge and devotion to truth is the hero of today. The world is avid for more information. The press, the radio, and television are set up as organs to satisfy the hunger of the mind. In theory, at least, the value of truth is recognized, and its beauty and changelessness appeal to men. It is "a fair and durable thing," an "evergreen" (*siempre verde*), with

> Such a face and such a mien,
> As to be loved needs only to be seen (Dryden).

The truth about God, about the world, and its history, about the nature of man, and man's destiny, about life and about our fellow men, and above all about ourselves, is what we look for instinctively. Truth convinces in the end; "it is the best argument." There is that in truth which proves itself to be so. Ben Jonson summed up the "self-justification" of truth in a quatrain:

Truth is the trial of itself,
And needs no other touch,
And purer than the purest gold,
Refine it ne'er so much.

To men of faith there is a motive more powerful than reason for admiring and loving truth. The motive lies in the person and example of Christ, who came to teach and spread the love of truth and who proclaimed: "I am . . . the Truth." He gave us the fundamental reason for being always loyal to truth, when He said: "The truth will make you free!"

Truth is an essential good and man needs it. Man needs truth more than he needs any other thing. Apart from the Divine Truth on which man's ultimate destiny depends, he needs truth, natural, discoverable truth, for ordinary living. He needs truth about what he may eat and what he may do with safety; he needs truth to conduct his business, his social relations with his fellow men. The administration of justice, precautions against disaster, and so forth, are all dependent on the acquisition and dissemination of truth. Life would soon be snarled if falsehood were substituted for truth. To change the sign-posts at street crossings, or the hands of clocks, or the dates on contracts, from fact to fiction, would lead to many a catastrophe. Only on the basis of truth can life go on.

Father Leslie Walker, S.J., sums up the simple argument for truth. "Since man is a social animal, naturally one owes to another that without which human society could not go on. But men could not live together if they did not believe one another to be speaking the truth. Hence the virtue of veracity comes to some extent under the head of justice (*rationem debiti*). The second source of the obligation to veracity arises from the fact that speech is clearly of its very nature intended for the communication of knowledge by one to another. It should be used therefore for the purpose for which it is naturally intended and lies should be avoided. For lies are not merely a misuse, but an abuse of the gift of speech. By destroying man's instinctive belief in the veracity of his neighbor, lies tend to destroy the efficacy of the gift of speech" (*Catholic Encyclopedia*, "Truth").

St. Paul lays down very clearly the moral law about lying. "Lie not to one another," he said (Col. 3:9), and again: "Wherefore putting away lying, speak ye the truth, every man to his neighbor." We know in our hearts that it is wrong to lie and that a lie is followed by a feeling of shame and a disturbed conscience. "Truth hath a quiet breast," says Shakespeare; there is no dishonor in it. Lord Chesterfield wrote to his son, out of his wide experience of life: "Remember then, as long as you live, that nothing but strict truth can carry you through the world, with either your conscience or your honor unwounded." And society, as we know, by the laws it enacts against perjury and practices of falsehood in business and in contracts, sanctions truth, and proclaims its necessity for the common good. As regards truthfulness, society is emphatically on the side of the moral law.

It is hardly necessary to define a lie, or to distinguish between a material and a formal lie. A man may say something which he believes to be true, and he may say it with the intention of conveying the truth, and yet the thing he says is in contradiction with actual fact. Such a lie is a material lie, but not a formal one, as the man is at heart, and in intent, truthful. A formal lie consists in "speaking against one's mind," speaking so as to deceive or to convey something other than the truth. It is being "double-minded" and "double-tongued." It involves injuring another by misleading him; it is essentially dishonorable, disrespectful to another.

"Lying," says Socrates, "infects the soul with evil." It is a practice which is associated with every kind of crime and wrongdoing. The man who is about to rob you, lies to you; the man who is about to kill you, lies to you. "Sin has many tools," wrote O. W. Holmes, "but a lie is the handle which fits them all." Treacherous men have no use for truth:

> For truth is precious and divine,
> Too rich a pearl for carnal swine (Sam Butler).

Lying begets lies. Tell one lie and soon you will find yourself obligated to tell more lies to substantiate the first. "A lie begets a lie till they come to generations." Whereas "the language of truth is simple," "a false tale needs a long preamble." The liar elaborates on his lie, trying to put it across and to make it more convincing. His assurances grow in strength and frequency. "A liar is always lavish of oaths" (Corneille). He has need of "a good memory," as St. Jerome said, to keep in mind all the details of the false story he tells. But in the end he is sure to be found out. "A lie never lives to be old," wrote Sophocles. The liar condemns himself and is soon recognized for what he is. He is discredited, despised. Thereafter he will not be believed even when he tells the truth. If you "use your head" you will never lie. "Wisdom never lies!"

But it is not always easy to tell the truth. We find ourselves in positions where we will hurt our friends, or hurt ourselves, if we tell the truth. The early Christian martyr exemplified the supreme test that truth-telling imposes. "Are you a Christian?" He was bound in conscience to answer truthfully that he was a Christian, knowing that death by torture would follow. In the witness box, the witness is asked, under oath, if he saw his brother or his friend at the scene of the crime. He is bound to answer truthfully, cost what it may. We may not tell a lie to hold on to a job, or to secure a good price for a piece of property, or to avoid being misunderstood and misrepresented. A lie, however immediately advantageous, will make you a slave; the truth, however immediately disadvantageous, will "make you free." Truth costs; we must not close our eyes to the fact. As John Wolcot wrote:

'Tis a narrow lane all full of quags,
Leading to broken heads, abuse and rags.

The commonest origin of the habit of lying is found in vanity, in self-advertisement. Having a fine idea of our own worth, and craving the admiration of others, we set out to glorify ourselves and in so doing we cease to be factual. We become downright liars.

We can trace the genesis of lying back to the prattle of children. Adoring parents listen to the "I," "I," "I," of their offsprings' tales. They encourage them by smiles and approbation to exaggerate and to boast about their doings. They know that their children are departing from the truth; they encourage them to do so! Meanwhile they nurture vanity and pride in their children, instead of modesty and humility. Later on in life, at school and subsequently at college, the children, now somewhat grown up, pursue the policy of self-advertisement, through the co-operation of lying. Next comes greed into the economy of life and in order to get things, and to retain possession of things acquired, recourse is had to lying.

As a contrast to the sad tale of parental folly, let me recount a story from my own life, a story to the credit of my mother. She was a widow, still very young and very beautiful, gentle, sweet tempered, but wise in having a care for the souls as well as the bodies of her three sons. Of one thing she was convinced, and she was prepared to act up to her conviction: *"The mouth that lies slays the soul."*

It happened that my brothers and I, all in our early

teens, had received a present of a cricket set — and we were very fond of playing cricket. Mother thought there was a little danger in cricket but still she always allowed us to play.

Well, the day after the cricket set came, my oldest brother happened to open the morning paper on the breakfast table. There we read, in bold headlines on the front page: "MAN KILLED AT CRICKET." We feared that we would not be allowed to play with our new set if Mother read the paper. My eldest brother, we others consenting, *hid the newspaper!*

When Mother come down to breakfast she asked where the paper was and my brother said: "I don't know!" It was an equivocation. He had closed his eyes as he threw the paper into an unused room.

Mother suspected something and insisted on his telling about the paper. When she found out about our being involved in a lie she flushed and then went pale. I had never seen her really angry before. She told us to carry our new cricket set down into the kitchen. There, in the great kitchen fireplace she made a bonfire of the bats, wickets, balls, and all. As the flames leaped and roared around our cherished playthings, she looked at us and said: "Never, never again, as long as you live, tell a lie!"

It was a terrible lesson, terribly sincere, and *terribly true!*

Often we excuse what we call "little lies," so-called "equivocations." But inasmuch as honest truth is departed from in equivocating, are we not acting dishonorably?

William Penn gave a grim warning: "Equivocation is half-way to lying, as lying is the whole way to hell." St. Alphonsus Liguori, an erstwhile lawyer, had such a horror of equivocation, that when a bishop was appointed to his diocese, who had shown himself hostile to the Redemptorists, St. Alphonsus would not write to congratulate him. He doubted that he could with complete veracity say: "I rejoice to hear of your Lordship's appointment." He knew that he and his Order would suffer as a result of his lack of "diplomacy," but the saint loved truth above security.

Are there liars who are not thieves? Can you rob your neighbor of his right to the truth without, at some time or other, robbing him of his material property? It may be that some pronounced liars avoid becoming thieves, but they have the wisdom of a well-known proverb against their chance of remaining honest: "Show me a liar and I will show you a thief!" The mentality of the liar is to take a ready and easy way out of difficulties; the robber has the same thing in mind.

While pride and greed are main sources of lying, servile fear is also a common source. Instead of being glad and proud to tell the truth and to remain free, we use lies and flatteries to placate or to win the protection of people of importance. We are, of course, under no obligation "to spill out" to everybody everything we know. Often it is wise and right to keep tight-lipped about things, "to keep our mouths shut." Especially should we be silent when we know things to the discredit of others.

It is right to remember: "Silence is never written down." Charity bids us guard the secrets of others as far as we can. "Do not tell everything but never lie," wrote Lord Chesterfield. Above all is a lie shameful and dishonorable when it is told through fear.

Any man who aims at living a life of honor has no choice whatsoever but to eschew lying and to hate lies. Lying runs counter to prudence, to justice, and to courage. It means "running away" from a spot of trouble; it means "playing it unfairly"; it means "not using one's head." To lie, also, is to lack respect for the rights of others, to make little of one's brother. The man of honor is apt to use Shakespeare's words:

> I had rather seal my lips than, to my peril,
> Speak that which is not!

Many readers will say, at this point, "Nice, of course, but *utterly unrealistic!*" Those readers will be lawyers, doctors, salesmen and saleswomen, receptionists, beauticians, secretaries, hostesses, politicians, and others. Each of them will think the same thought: "The rule of honor —never lie! — is O.K. in theory, but it is impossible in practice. I tell lies everyday, because I have to! I couldn't get on without lying!" Were one of them, a salesman, for example, to voice his thought to me I should answer him by asking a few questions.

First, I would ask him: "Did you ever try seriously to get along without telling lies?"

Second: "Are you sure that 'getting by' at the expense of your honor is worth while?"

Third: "Is it likely that a universal moral law, like that prohibiting lying — God's law — is unrealistic?"

Fourth: "If you have a young son whom you love, are you going to advise him to tell lies on the grounds that he will not be able to succeed in life unless he is a thorough liar?"

Fifth: "If lying, as Socrates taught, 'infects the soul with evil,' are you still going to teach your son (and your daughter, if you have one) to make their way in life by telling lies?"

There are certain classes of people from whom, unhappily, it is unwise to expect the truth. Among these, debtors come first. What they say and what they promise deserve little credence. "Lying rides on debts' back," says an adage. Then, we have those who are infatuated about something or who are in love. Of the latter Benjamin Franklin said humorously: "If Jack's in love, he is no judge of Jill's beauty." Those who talk a very great deal are also likely to lose track of truth. "Who speaks sows; who keeps silence reaps." It is not all good words and true that "talkers" sow, for "Good words are scarcer than emeralds."

The rule of honor and virtue — never lie! — is not as difficult and impractical as many think, but it requires, apart from love of truth, self-restraint in conversation. We must be inclined to say less rather than more and to watch closely what we are saying. If a lie slips over our lips we must catch up with it at once and change it into exact truth, at whatever cost to our self-esteem. "Truth is the daughter of God" (*La verdad es hija de Dios*), and we must never disown her. It is best for us to speak and live in accord with truth, for it cannot be hidden: "Like oil it comes to the top"; nor can it easily be interred. As the saying goes: "It takes a good many shovelfuls of earth to bury the truth!"

CHAPTER

IX

DON'T QUIT SCHOOL!

AMONG our friends we find some who admit readily: "I never read a book!" They are nice, busy people, but usually not *very* interesting. Their outlook is a little confined. Their remarks do not go very deep, and they are not informative, save about small practical matters. They say the same things again and again; and their ideas never change. Of such the Spaniards say: "*Quien poco sabe presto lo reza*" — He that knows little soon repeats it.

How "cocksure" people are who refrain from reading the thoughts and views of others! How certain they are about everything! The last thing they have a doubt about is their own infallibility! "He that knows nothing, doubts nothing!"

Yet there are people of this kind who respect knowledge though they run away from it. They would even like to know history and all about literature and science, but they are afraid to pay the price of knowing. "All wish to know but none to pay the fee." Abstentionists from the wine of wisdom, they prefer to rest secure and cozy in their "know-nothing" state. Are they not like cats who "love fish but are afraid to wet their paws"?

The greatly loved and witty Will Rogers has much to answer for. He set a pattern that too many Americans follow when he boasted: "All I know is what I read in the papers!" No doubt, Will Rogers read the papers pretty fully, whereas those who follow his ideal of self-education read only a few parts of the papers, the "sports" section and the "comic" strips. Women, many of whom are also followers of Rogers' educational theory, are not so keen about "sports" and "comics" but glance instead at "social columns" and advertising pages.

Many Americans keep away from books because they associate "book reading" with thinking, and they are emphatically hostile to thinking, especially "serious thinking." They have no palate for thought as such, and they regard it as the hardest and most forbidding kind of work. T. A. Edison, who lived long among us and knew us well, said: "There is no expedient to which a man will not go to avoid the real labor of thinking." And so, instead of reading, which sits cheek by jowl with thinking, we talk, we "chew the rag." "I like to talk," said someone, "because when I'm talking I don't have to think!"

As we follow the normal course of living we pass from grammar school to high, from high to college, from college to a job of some kind. Thus we change from one locale to another, but in so doing our basic need does not change. Our years within the walls of learning were meant as a preliminary preparation for the good life, but the need of being fit to live well and honorably survives the laying down of our schoolbooks. We still remain unready, unfinished, with minds only half built and half furnished. Nevertheless the idea is abroad that the quest of knowledge is officially over when we depart from the schoolroom. People do not see that the mind is land that continues to need cultivation. As Cicero wrote: "As a field however fertile cannot be fruitful without cultivation, neither can a mind without learning."

As Christians we are accustomed to consider the gifts that God bestows upon us, among which the mind and reason are outstanding, as *talents* to be put to use and developed. We know from Scripture how grave a thing it is "to bury a talent." Should it not be clear to us that it is no light fault on our part when we allow our minds to starve and sicken?

Reason is given us not only for our own good but also for the good of others. Education has a social purpose; its motive should not only be self-perfection but love of others. We cannot play a fair and honorable part in life, as mature humans, unless we possess "well-fed" minds as well as strong hands. Are we playing it fair with our neighbors if we only serve them with inferior instruments? Are we to assist others with hands only, not with our minds? Are we fully charitable when we share gold alone, and not knowledge? "Desire for knowledge is the path of honor," wrote an Arabian sage. Always we should be learning, pursuing truth, whatever the source of knowledge may be. One does well "to learn from the mole to plough and from the worm to weave."

Now, a good man will say to me: "Sure, learning is a fine thing. It's good to learn. But, it's not in my line. I get on very well without studying and reading books. I leave that kind of things to others. Frankly, I can't be bothered."

There are reasons, however, which justify the pursuit of learning and they can be applied to persons of every temperament and of every age. For one thing, the man of knowledge is less inclined to be lonely, his vision is peopled with persons and places and actions. Learning is "a good companion," and, as the saying goes, "A good companion on a journey is worth a coach."

Knowledge, too, means power; it means riches, and better, for it replaces riches. Solon, who was among the wisest of men, increased his wealth with his years. "I grow old learning something new every day," he said. Our knowledge does not die and cannot be stolen from us; it is always at hand and available for use. "The learned man has always riches in himself," wrote Phaedrus. And there is a thought that has taken shape in many literatures which reminds us that when all material things are lost we still have our precious learning.

> When house and land are gone and spent,
> Then learning is most excellent (S. Foote, 1752).

What are we to think of a man who "hates anything serious" and whose only mental pabulum is "light stuff," snippets from digests and "quicky" magazines? On what does his mind feed? On bran? Surely not on flour! "Who shuns the mill, shuns the flour." What becomes of the mind when it never gets good bread to eat?

Francis Bacon, whose knowledge was encyclopedic, thought very poorly of those who were content to be ignorant. No doubt in the Courts of Elizabeth and James there were many such — and perhaps they were jealous of him. He spoke truly, if sourly, when he said: "A man is but what he knoweth!" If it be true to say of a farmer that his land is worth what he is worth as a man, it is no less true to say of a host that his feast is worth, not the wines and viands that are on the table, but "the reason and flow of soul" that is exchanged between himself and his guests.

"*What is the great end of learning?*" The answer is given in the same language, though with different emphasis, by Christian and pagan philosophy. The answer, which merits deep thought, is: "*To seek for the lost mind.*"

As we learn we search. We look for truth, ultimate truth. When we find It we are come upon God. There we find ourselves in God, in Light and in Life. The finding of "the lost mind" is the finding of God, revealed through knowledge. Very beautifully St. Paul (Eph. 5:8, 9) advises us: "Walk ye as children of the light; for the fruit of light is in all goodness and justice and truth!"

In a lesser way, in finding "the lost mind" we find our better selves, the selves that are open to inspiration, to

adventure, to exhilaration. In knowledge we realize another, newer kind of delight, that of fresh ideas. "A poor
scholar," say the Chinese, "accepts no pity." He has no
need of pity! He is richer, better off, than the mandarin
that rides proudly by!

For all his fanaticism, Mohammed said many things
with imagination and insight. Though no scholar himself,
he saw the worth and the promise of learning. One of
the utterances attributed to him reveals this reverence.
"The ink of the scholar," he said, *"is more holy than the
blood of the martyr."* Who can tell whether Aquinas' ink
or Sebastian's blood merits more in God's eyes?

In the matter of choosing books to read all is not plain
sailing. How and where are we to find a right book? There
is a remarkable proverb from Italy which merits quoting
in the original: *"Non v'è il peggior ladro d'un cattivo
libro"* — There is no worse robber than a bad book.

Libraries are filled with two kinds of tenants: thieves
and honest men. The thieves also are of two kinds: the
harmless and the harmful. The former are books by writ-
ers who have nothing worth while to say but "who leave
nothing in their inkstands." They rob us of our time, and
that is bad enough. The harmful thieves steal both our
time and part of our souls if we let them do so. Out of a
book "the bee sucks honey, the spider poison." If we
have the disposition of spiders we need to beware of
harmful robbers.

In reading a great classic of the past, we have the seal
of approval set on the masterpiece by the human race. A

classic survives as such on account of some undeniable worth in it. From it there is "honey to be sucked" and light to be gained. Then we have the experience of having our eyes opened: "Dead men open living men's eyes!"

I have already suggested that people of all temperaments and all ages keep on learning. Did I mean to include those who are aged? Should old men and elderly women still read and study? Why not? "One is never too old to learn!"

Memories of the best and most beautiful library I ever visited still linger in my mind. The Kildare Street Library in the heart of Dublin (the city where, in my day, even the "cabbies" knew Greek and Latin) was always thronged. A large portion of the eager students, both men and women, were old and gray. One could see them *waiting for their books*, for they had to be sought for from top shelves and obscure corners. It was not the "comics" that the gray heads of Dublin read!

It is told of an ancient Greek, Lacydes by name, that at a very great age he set about mastering geometry. When his inquisitive friends inquired of him why, at his age, he was learning geometry, he gave an answer that became a proverb. *"When, if not now?"* Lacydes dared not postpone his adventure!

Michaelangelo, as an old man, but still a searcher after knowledge, created an artistic figure of an ancient with an hourglass, saying: *"Ancora imparo"* — I am still learning.

But is it a practical adventure for an old man to set

out on a new hunt for knowledge? I cannot speak for others, only for myself . . . and that briefly, for I'm no great Nimrod in the field.

My fancy was suddenly caught, not long ago, by some witty and wise "sayings" — "ye olde sayed saws" — and the hunt for others and others began. These "copper coins of human wisdom" are full of color and humor. They have survived for untold ages on account of their truth and the perfection with which they record the thoughts and feelings of the human race. Books upon books have been written about them, and innumerable collections of them have been made.

But the pleasure they give! The surprises they afford! They cover every phase of men's ways and men's fortunes with a quiet smile. The unlucky man, they tell you, "hurts his nose when he falls on his back." Of the smiling villain they say: "Even the worst dog wags his tail!" Or: "A wild goose never lays a tame egg." And so on. The oldest eyes should glow and be merry over books to the last!

There is, of course, a great difference between "lovers of learning" and "lovers of words." The latter feel no real reverence for knowledge; they "bandy" words about, which too often they do not properly understand. The "lover of learning" tries to go deep into a matter, to grasp it fully and clearly, as it were "to come to know his friend as well as he can." The other, "the lover of words," is content with a "smattering" about a thing. His grasp of a subject is insecure and deceptive. "He hasn't got the eel who holds it by the tail!"

"The lover of words" makes a great display of such learning as he has. He shows off and tries to impress people. His attitude is one of vainglory. Chesterfield issued a quaint warning to such exhibitionists: "Wear your learning like your watch, in a private pocket."

When we are ignorant of something about which we are questioned we should not attempt to conceal our ignorance in a plethora of words. Good sense and humility suggest that we confess our limitations saying: "I don't know," without explaining, at length, about all we do know but how that particular matter escaped us. It is refreshing to read the lines of Allan Ramsay (1721):

> For when I dinna clearly see
> I always own I dinna ken
> An' that's the way o' wisest men.

To pretend to great knowledge is a mark of ignorance, for any well-informed man should see clearly the narrow bounds of his learning. Every man's knowledge is both subjective and inexact. "He that boasts of his own knowledge proclaims his ignorance." The only safe boast to make is that of Socrates: "I know nothing except the fact of my ignorance."

It may be to the point to refer to a few of the unfortunate consequences of "quitting school" and putting aside all further interest in learning.

There is, for instance, the ugly phenomenon of immigrants to this country who neglect to learn our language properly. They are well received and well treated. They enjoy equal privileges with all citizens. But through fear of studying, or through sheer laziness, they never learn to speak perfect English. Everyone in contact with them *suffers* as a result of their "quitting school"!

There is next the disquieting phenomenon of the ignorant, uninformed Christian, whose duty it is to be a bulwark of faith in God and of good morals. Catholic or Protestant, he "never reads a book," and he remains unable to defend religion and revelation, when scoffers assail principles dear to him. The Christian who remains ignorant of his creed makes a sheep of himself. Does he not know: "Who makes himself a sheep, the wolf devours him!" To be specific, the Catholic man who is afraid "to tire his head" by reading, and studying so that he can thoroughly understand the tenets of his faith, and defend them with solid reasons, has neither "guts" nor an enlightened outlook on life.

Sometimes a Catholic, carried away by feeling, enters an argument with a learned agnostic only to be easily worsted on account of his ignorance. If such a Catholic has not learning, let him at least have some wit. Let him ponder the old Spanish adage: "Don't talk Arabic in the house of a Moor!"

There is a third important class of people to whom the advice — "don't quit school!" — should strike home. The class is that of parents who have the responsibility of *educating* their children. They love their children; why do they let them down by choosing to remain ignorant? It is a primordial truth: "A loved child requires teaching!" And from where is the teaching to come, if not from the parents? No doubt some of the teaching may be deputized, but not all of it, and certainly not the important part of it.

Fathers and mothers would like to help their children at their studies — and to follow intelligently their children's efforts "to keep up with their classes." But unless they equip themselves in time, how can they do so? If they find themselves despised by their children for their ignorance of general facts of history, literature, and science, their repentance will come too late. "When the well's dry we know the worth of water." When we are hurt on account of our ignorance, we know the worth of knowledge.

That it is the part of honor to cultivate the mind and to keep it cultivated should be clear to all. If we have been remiss about our studies we can easily begin again. Anacreon's saying: "By trying you shall learn," can be reversed to good purpose so as to read: "You can learn if you try!" Trying brings about everything; trying to fill up the empty places in the mind with solid knowledge will bring results.

It is the way of honor to "nourish the arts" — to perfect our spiritual abilities. The mind can be turned from a piece of wasteland into a garden where lovely flowers grow. And the gardener will find that as flowers beget flowers, thoughts beget thoughts — he will happily discover "more sprigs in his garden than ever he sowed."

CHAPTER

X

KEEP SHAME ALIVE!

THERE are two kinds of shame: true shame and false shame. The former is healthy and a blessing; the latter is unhealthy and a curse. The injunction — "keep shame alive!" — refers to true shame because it is closely related to honor.

True shame is rarely appreciated at its proper value. It is the intimate and delicate reaction of a noble soul. It becomes a man of honor and is "his glory and his grace" (Eccles.) To it the proverb refers, which says: "Where there is no shame there is no honor!"

False shame, on the other hand, is the reaction of vain and silly minds. It is the outcome of pride and of fear — of fear of what people may say or think. It is often acutely painful — a veritable torture — but the pain and torture are unnecessary and to no purpose. In false shame there is so much absurdity and cowardice that it is far removed from honor.

Bernard Shaw, who equated false shame with "respectability," laid down the paradox: "The more things people are ashamed of the more respectable they are." Enlarging on "respectability," he continued: "We live in an atmosphere of shame. We are ashamed of everything that is real about us; ashamed of ourselves; of our relations; of our incomes; of our accents; of our opinions; of our experiences; just as we are ashamed of our naked skins."

It is true, as Shaw says, that we are ashamed "of everything that is real about us"; of our gray hairs and age; of our height, if we are very small or very tall; of our weight, if we are fat; of our warts or pimples or wigs or false teeth.

We are ashamed of our relations, if they are unfortunate or eccentric, and would like to hide them away rather than that our friends should meet them or know about them.

If we are poor, we are ashamed of our incomes and attempt to create the impression that we are richer than we are. We suffer deprivations to "keep up appearances." Some of us "put everything on our backs and nothing in our bellies," lest neighbors should know that we are hard up. "The Devil," wrote Benjamin Franklin, "wipes his breech with poor folks' pride."

Like the nightingale of fiction, "that dies of shame if another bird sings better," we suffer cruel pangs when we are outclassed in our particular specialty. We cannot bear to play "second fiddle" or to be beaten in a contest.

The shame of defeat is intolerable to us, even when we are defeated through no fault of our own. If our business venture fails, we are ashamed; if we lose an election, we are ashamed; if we are put off a team or turned down in an examination, we are ashamed. The bitter shadow of pride follows us everywhere, whiplashing us. As Piers Plowman said: "There smites nothing so sharp, nor smelleth so sour, as shame!"

How infinite are the ramifications of false shame! A young man at a party inadvertently spills a plate of soup over the tablecloth. His embarrassment and distress — over nothing — is pitiable to see. A smart girl discovers, when halfway down Fashion Row, that she has a run in her nylons and that others are noticing it. She winces with shame. How much poor humanity suffers on account of false shame!

This kind of suicidal shame does more than hurt humans; it leads them astray. "It is the false shame of fools," wrote Horace, "which tries to cover unhealed sores." There are patients who, through shame, only tell half the story to their doctors; clients who conceal from their lawyers the darker aspects of their cases; penitents, in confession, who gloss over or guiltily hide grave sins. Such patients, clients, and penitents *hurt themselves* because they are subservient to false shame. And, all the time, that shame is but an illusion, a concoction of the mind!

Such is the prevalence of false shame that we take for granted that everyone is liable to it. One woman will glance, meaningfully, at another woman's shoes or hat to embarrass her. A teacher will, as a punishment, make a child stand in the corner of the classroom, knowing the child will be hurt by shame. The blackmailer has, in many cases, only to threaten a "revelation" in order to be paid off. The State *increases* the punishment of convicts by various forms of degradation, provocative of shame, although such penalties are not explicitly imposed by judge or jury.

During World War I patriotic women took it upon themselves to present "white feathers" to young men of military age whom they saw in the streets. They regarded them as guilty of cowardice and counted on "shame" as a method of reform. "Those who fear not guilt yet start at shame," says a proverb. They hoped to force them into the army by making them ashamed.

Sometimes, these self-appointed recruiting sergeants made mistakes. One lady, in Trafalgar Square (London), handed a young man who *looked* like a slacker a "white feather." He took it from her with his right hand and with his left hand he took out a glass eye and offered it in exchange. The lady fell down in a dead faint!

If a false shame were caused by our guilt there would be some excuse for it. "It is the crime which makes the shame, not the scaffold," wrote Corneille. But we are unconcerned about our guilt and care only about what people may say of us. It is the fear of being despised that motivates false shame. If we are caught listening at a door, or reading a letter that belongs to another, it is not the fact that we have violated the rights of another that makes us ashamed, but the fact that someone has seen our meanness and our treachery.

To lessen our habit of feeling false shame, two things are necessary. First, we should learn to recognize facts as facts. Second, we should prefer humility to pride.

If it be a *fact* that we are poor or cross-eyed or stupid, we must *accept the fact* and thank God for it, rather than repine over it or attempt to conceal it. We may have a brother in Sing Sing, or an uncle in a madhouse, and that others should learn about such facts and comment upon them should not worry us or cause us any embarrassment. Why should the thoughts and words of others, which we can never evaluate, frighten or distress us? Why let others be in control of our peace of soul?

As regards humility, namely, the sensible and lowly value we should put upon ourselves, it is always a friend and a protector. It saves us from make-belief and false-hood and all the cares that arise therefrom. Pride, on the other hand, which motivates false shame, befuddles us and injures us. It is our worst enemy.

> Of all the causes that conspire to blind
> Man's erring judgment and misguide his mind,
> What the weak head with strongest bias rules,
> It's pride, the never-failing vice of fools (Alex. Pope).

Turning now to *true shame*, we find it described as "the loveliest of all sweet passions." Though rarely appreciated, as I have said, it should be studied and cultivated by all.

To quote the proverb, for a second time: "Where there is no (true) shame there is no honor!"

When we see someone commit an act of cruelty or injustice we say, instinctively: "He ought to be ashamed of himself!" In so saying we betray recognition of what true shame is. We recognize that one guilty of crime should feel within himself a sense of unworthiness and remorse. It is not "hurt pride" or embarrassment that we expect of him, but the spontaneous beginnings of repentance.

It is not common to witness true shame. Often we see people blush, hide their faces, and stammeringly attempt "to explain" when they have done something wrong. But stammering, hiding, and blushing are more often signs of injured vanity and of an appeal for sympathy than of true shame. "I never wonder," wrote Jonathan Swift, "to see men wicked, but I often wonder to see them not ashamed!"

Is there a sign of shame more convincing than blushing and hiding away? Aristotle answered this question in the affirmative. He wrote: *"The eyes are the abode of shame!"* What Aristotle meant was that true shame expresses itself in sincere tears.

If we search the Gospel for the doctrine of true shame we find the story of the Prodigal and the story of Magdalen. The Prodigal did not hide away in self-pity, but came home, humbly and boldly, to his father. He confessed his unworthiness — no doubt there were tears in his eyes — but he was unafraid. He did not stammer or blush or stand silent with downcast head. He didn't "play-act" to excite sympathy. His sense of guilt, his sorrow therefor, even his "confusion" of soul, were sincere and simple. His was true shame!

Magdalen, like the Prodigal, instead of hiding away and blushing, came boldly (and humbly) to Christ and wept at His feet. Her consciousness of guilt and her acute sorrow for her crimes found expression in tears. Also she expressed her inner feeling in an act of generosity. With precious ointment she anointed Christ's feet.

True shame has fine qualities. It is not the outcome of fear, like false shame, but of courage. It is just, reasonable, temperate. It ennobles the one who cherishes it. In Magdalen we can see the meaning of the poetic line; quoted above: "Shame is the loveliest of all sweet passions."

When a man of honor repents for an evil deed, when he feels sure that God has forgiven it, he still clings to his sense of shame for having done wrong. He regards his shame as a valuable, sobering aftermath. He guards it not only as a memory, but as an active factor in his soul.

Some people would willingly rid themselves of all shame for past wrongdoing. "Better forget about it!" they say. "What's past is past! It's unhealthy to keep alive in consciousness that sense of sorrow and humility!" The poet Prior moodily bewails the fact that shame continues even after the sin is absolved:

> No penance can absolve our guilty fame,
> Nor tears, that wash out sin, can wash out shame!
>
> (Matthew Prior.)

There are, however, good and convincing reasons why we should not wish or try to rid ourselves of the lingering shame we feel over one or all of our past misdeeds. Shame, more than anything else, helps us to *feel* and *realize* the evil and dishonor in the wrongs we committed, and protects us against their recurrence.

We should not, of course, allow others to know about this sacred, inner reaction of our souls. It is between us and God. It is felt in the presence of God, before His all-seeing eye. Shame becomes more acute in proportion to its being cherished as worship of God.

Shame should be cultivated. We should deliberately recall to mind the occasion of that misdeed of ours which more than any other made us feel true shame. And we should nurture that feeling and make it more intense.

In one of the most telling meditations of the *Spiritual Exercises,* that on "the three sins," St. Ignatius Loyola, a master of spiritual living, instructs his readers *to pray for shame and confusion* in the face of their sins. He tells them to take pains to turn over in their minds such reflections as will induce shame. From his knowledge and experience of chivalry he recognized in shame a saving reaction, a sobering influence.

The good man who does wrong and repents, with shame in his heart, does not lose his stature. He remains greater than lesser men who may not have sinned as he sinned. He is still a diamond; they are but pebbles. "Better," says the proverb, "a diamond with a flaw than a pebble without one."

It should not be thought, from what has been written about shame that it is essentially emotional and negative. Shame is fostered by the mind and will, and is provocative of action.

If we look back over our lives we will find, no doubt, in our misconduct, some instance of gross ingratitude, or some act whereby we inflicted hurt on innocent people. When we study the wantonness and ugliness of what we have done we may not *feel* in our senses any emotional reaction, but what we do feel is mental abhorrence. We say to ourselves: "I would not act in that way if I could live my life over again. What a hideous person I was to act so!"

Such a state of mind, if sincere, is the basis of shame, but it is still a negative state. What next? In what manner does shame become active?

The person toward whom we have been ungrateful, or whom we have injured, may be alive. So, to make amends, we take steps to undo the past by present action. We "make up for the past" in every way that occurs to us. Our shame is now creative. It is genuine virtue; it becomes, as we have said, "our glory and our grace."

We should not be ashamed, as we have said above, to have to confess our ignorance and say: "I dinna ken!" We should not be ashamed over being beaten in a game or over some gaucherie that causes others to laugh at us. If our friends are poor or in trouble we should not avoid them, lest we be thought little of. The Chinese remind us with delicacy that "a dog is not averse to a poor home."

It is their nice way of saying: "Don't be ashamed of friends who have no money to pay for a nice house."

If we are ashamed of our physical defects, of our big ears or big feet, we are being stupid; but when we are ashamed of having "talked big," or in our gluttony emptied big tankards, we are being wise. Let us reserve our shame for the occasions when we hurt others and act dishonorably, not for the occasions when our petty sensibilities are wounded. "When shame keeps its watch," wrote the great Edmund Burke, "virtue is not wholly extinguished in the heart!"

Shame will continue to watch while we "keep shame alive," and in watching it will guard our honor.

XI

SAY YOUR PRAYERS!

I HAVE tried to write the foregoing pages with complete sincerity. I have evaded no question that occurred to me, and I have answered honestly every question that arose in my discussion of honor. Now I have to face the most trying question of all — and the most important: "Can a man live a life of honor without the help of God?"

There were Socrates of old, and Cato, Seneca, and Brutus, who all, with an untold number of others, enjoyed the reputation of being honorable. There were heroes and leaders, beloved of their various countries. There were poets who taught virtue and patriotism. There was Vergil who was regarded as a pagan prophet of Christianity. We do not know how far God may have influenced and helped them in their lives; but I have no doubt, however hard it may be to say so, that unless God did help them, they fell far short of true honor. Such is my faith, such my personal conviction.

My thought is that of the good À Kempis. "There is no

wisdom, Lord, if You cease to guide! No courage if You cease to defend! No chastity is secure if You do not guard it! Our vigilance avails nothing if Your holy watchfulness does not protect us! Left to ourselves we sink and perish, but visited by You we are lifted up and live!" (Bk. III, ch. XIV.)

Honor is a spiritual achievement. It is something won by the efforts of the heart, mind, and will. It is not, as we know, an inherited gift, nor one come upon by chance, or discovered within oneself. It is a moral victory gained and maintained by a struggle.

The rules that I have outlined are the strategy to be followed in that struggle. They will help if they are observed but to observe them more than human effort is required. I would be deceiving my readers were I to pretend that anyone, however noble and determined, who relied upon himself alone, could keep these rules! To win true honor something in addition to high ideals and a firm will is necessary. *That something transcends the natural:* it is help, *grace,* obtained from God by prayer!

When a man relies on himself alone in his fight to overcome the promptings of pride or of fear, and the seductions of the senses, he inevitably fails in the end. The soul of man cannot for long resist with success the constant drag downward of bodily appetites. He grows weaker, poorer: "Covetousness hoards itself poor." Man's nature is fallen, corrupted, and tends to take the easy way of dishonor. Everyone who believes in God, whether Christian or Jew, knows this. Every believer knows the necessity of seeking and obtaining God's assistance. If God does not help one to build his house of honor, he "labors in vain who builds it."

As I write I look out at my dogs, resting in the afternoon sunshine in my hilltop garden. They are good dogs and faithful, my blue terrier and my red setter, "Bran." I love them dearly. "Hunger and ease," says an English proverb, "is a dog's life." My dogs have "ease and plenty" for their living — but they are Irish dogs.

They follow me through fields and valleys, night and morning; they chase "cottontails" and calves. "Bran" in his exhilaration leaps into the air in pursuit of birds that fly by. They cuddle near me, when evening comes and logs crackle in the fireplace. They look endearingly into my eyes, professing faith and honor — but, alas, when the test of honor arises, they fail! Their nature is splendid — throbbing with life and frolic — but temptation is too much for them. There are things that they can't resist; my table is the silent witness to many a theft. And I am unwilling witness to the proverb: "A dog in a kitchen likes to be alone." Between their honor and that which I can possess there lies a great gap — the gap that only prayer can bridge.

The man who would lead a life of honor must accept the duty of prayer. A "splendid nature," a gay spirit "throbbing with life and frolic," a galaxy of "endearing ways" do not suffice for man,

> If knowing God, he lifts not hands of prayer,
> Both for himself, and those who call him friend.

I do not mean here to attempt to define prayer, or to venture into the domain of theology. Suffice it to say that there are many, many forms of prayer, many methods of "raising the heart to God." Prayer, as James Montgomery writes, can be:

> The burden of a sigh,
> The falling of a tear:
> The upward glancing of an eye
> When none but God is near.

And prayer, let me add, is for everyone, saint and sinner alike. The man who is afraid to pray because he knows that he is in sin, is unmindful of the mercy and compassion of God. He is being foolish if he thinks that he should wait until he is sinless before praying. Never are any of us in this life wholly free from sin.

> Be not afraid to pray; to pray is right;
> Pray if thou canst with hope, but ever pray,
> Though hope be weak or sick with long delay;
> Pray in the darkness if there be no light!
> (Hartley Coleridge.)

All of us, Catholics, Protestants, Jews, are taught to pray with humility and faith; and we are taught to pray, not in a temple only, but anywhere, any time.

> Kneel down, remote, upon the simple sod,
> And sue, *in forma pauperis*, to God (T. Hood).

Again I repeat the question that everyone has a right to ask: "Can a man live a life of honor without the help of God?" Again, I answer with an emphatic: "No!"

Now, I ask the corollary question: "Can a man live a life of honor if he prays to God for help?" And to this question, I answer with an emphatic: "Yes!"

To those who believe in God there is nothing more certain than that He gives help in answer to prayer. "Prayer," wrote James Montgomery,

> Moves the arm which moves the world,
> And brings salvation down.

With the assistance that God gives in answer to prayer, perfect honor, perfect honesty, truthfulness, and justice are possible. "When the grace of God cometh unto a man, then he is able for all things," writes À Kempis. Prayer raises and inspires us to live on a high level of conduct, to fulfill our duties fully. Wrote the socialist and social reformer, Robert Owen, who was neither monk nor mystic: "He who prays as he ought, will endeavor to live as he ought."

There are some who have had little experience of the effects of prayer, and who perhaps, despairingly, look on prayer as a vague and superstitious exercise, a sentimental meandering among high clouds. Because they have not tasted it or been nourished by it, they think that spiritual food is a chimera. Because they have never had the courage to come close up to their heavenly Father, begging Him for bread, they conclude, with little logic, that others have never done so — that others have never felt joy and strength in contact with God!

When I meet a man who is blind I feel in my heart

a great pity for him and a deep sympathy with him. I know how great a loss it is never to see a friend's face, never to watch the sheep on a hillside. But I take some comfort for his sake from the fact that *he knows that he is blind* — and that he can pray with humility: "Lord, that I may see!" He does not refuse my arm to lead him across the street, he is not so proud or mad as to say: "Get away! I can see as well as you!"

Then, I feel pity too, a deeper pity, a more poignant sympathy, for the atheist, whose bodily eyes are sound, but whose mental eyes have lost their vision. In his case I get no comfort from the fact that he knows that he is blind. Alas, he does not know it! He is *dark* but he believes his darkness is light. He prays not: "Lord, that I may see!" Instead, he says to me: "Poor fellow! It is you who are blind!" There is nothing I can do for him; he will not allow me to lead him across a street.

In his recent book, *The Hidden Stream*, Father Ronald Knox says: "Few things are so disappointing in life as the experience gradually borne in upon one, that it is very difficult in real life to convince people by the arguments which seem satisfactory to oneself."

Turning now to a very practical question that may well concern any one of us — what if I lose my honor? What if I become a thief? What if I perjure myself? What if I become a traitor? Can I ever again recover my lost honor? Can failure and shame be converted into triumph and chivalry?

Boileau, the French poet, describing honor as a rocky

isle, says: "Once one has abandoned it (honor) one can never return." In other words, he teaches that when we fall into disgrace we are ruined forever.

Boileau, no doubt, had in mind that "outer honor" of which I have spoken; that "fame of repute" that exists outside the self, in the thoughts and minds of other men. He who loses his good name in the public eye, by some act of treachery, is *usually* "blasted" forever. The traitor is followed with a suspicious eye; as Shakespeare put it: "Treason is trusted like a fox!"

"Outer honor," however, is of only relative importance. It is never a safe possession, never secure, and its loss, even when due to one's own misconduct, can be replaced by other and better things.

But what of the real honor, the "inner honor" that dwells in the heart? If it is lost through misconduct, can it be recovered? Can honor, true and bright, flourish on the ruins of its former habitation? To reduce the question to its proper religious status — can sin be forgiven, wholly and completely, and replaced by virtue?

In every religion there is some form of sacrament or atonement through which sin is forgiven, and peace of mind, self-respect, and virtue restored. The Catholic penitent, no matter how grievous his treachery and shame, finds in the sacrament of penance a full restoration of his former innocence and honor. Nay more, he finds himself, by reason of his repentance, possessed of still more honor than he ever enjoyed!

Such is "the way of God with men," the way of a Father who knows the frailty of His children.

"Outer honor," when once lost, *usually* is gone forever. There are nonetheless some well-known instances in history of the recovery of public glory after public shame. There is the instance of King David as told in the Bible; there is also the instance of St. Augustine as recorded in general history. In the Book of Wisdom, we have a fascinating analysis of "the just man." "He will open his mouth in prayer and *will seek pardon for his sins.*" Having recovered his honor as a result of prayer, "the memory of him shall not pass away and his name shall be in request from generation to generation." Prophetically we are taught that both "outer" and "inner" honor can be recovered.

Some of us there are who fall not once but again and again from honor, by our thefts or intemperance or other sins. Some of us are so frail that we seem only to be able to hold fast to innocence and honor for a brief spell at a time. Are we therefore wholly without honor?

Not so! There remains to us one strong claim to being men of honor. In spite of recurring defeat we keep on fighting, we keep on "seeking Christ in sorrow." Is there not high honor in such courage, in such perseverance?

The outstanding difference between a man of honor and a man without honor is that the former is not afraid of the light but rejoices in it, while the latter prefers the darkness — he is always in dread of detection.

This difference of outlook of the honest and the dishonest man was beautifully and perfectly revealed in the words that Christ spoke to Nicodemus when the latter came on a timorous visit to Christ by night. Christ told the learned doctor that "men love darkness rather than light for their works are evil."

Then Christ laid down in figurative language the definition of honor: "Everyone that doth evil hateth the light, and cometh not to the light, that his works may not be reproved. But he that doth truth, cometh to the light, that his works may be made manifest, because they are done in God."

The honorable man "has nothing to hide." The dishonorable man is always hiding something, and his honesty is suspect. "A vessel hidden under the cloak is seldom come by honestly." The honorable man leads only one life: he is that inwardly which he seems to be outside. The soul of his opposite is full of ugly secrets. The man of honor feels safe — he is safe! He is safe because his life is unblemished.

Once again we repeat the deep thought of Livy: *"Honor is most safe, because it is most beautiful."*

By instinct we pay tribute to honor. The tribute we pay is to seek for a hero whom we may sincerely worship. Like many another, in all my reading, I have searched for a hero, a man of honor, searched avidly until at last I found one that satisfied all my hopes.

My "man of honor," my hero, is the little "wandering

Jew" who fought and taught and suffered so long and so much: Paul of Tarsus. Courteous, patient, loving, and absolutely fearless before furious foes or in thundering storms, he went his way, "always rejoicing," "praying without ceasing," "comforting the feeble-minded," "supporting the weak," "following that which is good toward all men." Paul "played it fair," if anyone ever did. He "did his job"; he "paid his debts"; he "lied to no man."

Fearlessly and unequivocally, he proclaimed the despised doctrine of love and honor that Christ had taught. "I am not ashamed of the gospel," he wrote (Rom. 1:16), "for it is the power of God unto salvation."

He taught love — it was the main work of his life: love for all men without distinction, Greeks, Barbarians, Jews, and Gentiles. He was tolerant as he was humble, the willing slave of all. His eloquence, his brilliant intellect, his expansive heart that wept for his friends, his delicate thoughtfulness for the comfort and safety of others, his respect for others' rights, added glamour to the glory of this hero, "sans peur et sans reproche." And, above all, he remained faithful to the end, "finishing his course."

In Paul's letters we find a complete and perfect code of honor as we do of charity. "Lie not to one another." "Bear with one another." "Forgive one another." "Be not double-tongued." "Serve not to the eye." "Let love be without dissimulation." "Have peace with all men." "Work good to all men."

And then, this brave and noble hero, having told us what honor is, turns to us in his human way and asks us with a pathos that brings tears to our eyes: *"Am I become your enemy because I tell you the truth?"*

Who can deny, having read Paul's letters and studied Paul's life, that religion is the main and necessary bulwark of honor? Who can deny that the rule of honor that guarantees all the other rules is that which reads: "Say your prayers!" But while we pray for honor, for the grace to live honorably, we must never relax one iota of our purely human effort to "use our heads" and "play it fair." Our duty is not single, but double — it is both natural and supernatural — and it is summed up in the ancient saying:

Pray devoutly but hammer stoutly!

to which we say, "Amen."